uncovered editions

THE STRANGE STORY OF ADOLPH BECK

London: The Stationery Office

First published 1904 Cd. 2315
© Crown Copyright

This abridged edition
© The Stationery Office 1999
Reprinted with permission.

ISBN 0 11 702414 7

A CIP catalogue record for this book is available from the
British Library.

Printed in the UK by Biddles Limited, Guildford, Surrey
J93506   C50   11/99

THE STRANGE STORY OF ADOLPH BECK

uncovered editions

Titles in the series

SP 29/7/07

The Boer War: Ladysmith and Mafeking, 1900

Wilfrid Blunt's Egyptian Garden: Fox-hunting in Cairo

The British Invasion of Tibet: Colonel Younghusband, 1904

The Strange Story of Adolph Beck

The Loss of the Titanic, 1912

War 1914: Punishing the Serbs

R101: the Airship Disaster, 1930

War 1939: Dealing with Adolf Hitler

Tragedy at Bethnal Green, 1943

The Judgement of Nuremburg, 1946

Rillington Place

John Profumo & Christine Keeler, 1963

Uncovered Editions are historic official papers which have not previously been available in a popular form. The series has been created directly from the archive of The Stationery Office in London, and the books have been chosen for the quality of their story telling. Some subjects are familiar, but others are less well known. Each is a moment of history.

In 1895, Adolph Beck was arrested and convicted of the crimes of deception and larceny. The account given here is one of the strangest true stories in British legal history.

1877–1881

I, Ada Wooding, live at 8, Northway Road, Cambrian Road, Brixton. I am single. About four months ago I met prisoner between Charing Cross and Ludgate Hill. We had a conversation and he said he should like to see me again. He came to my address on the 8th March after I had received a letter from him. He said he had an offer to make me, and my house was not good enough for me, and he would keep me. He had a villa at St. John's Wood and I was to go there and have a servant, a page, and a little trap to go out in.

He brought out a cheque for £13 10s. and said I was too quiet, and I was to have different dresses and go for them to Howell and James. He would send his brougham for me between 6 and 7 o'clock, and I was to have some boxes and some jewellery. He also said my rings were not good enough. They were too thick and clumsy. He asked me to put them in an envelope and he would have a sapphire stone put in my wedding ring. The diamond ring was not good enough, and I put them in an envelope and let him take them because I believed the cheque to be good. He gave me the cheque before he took the jewellery. He said he'd broken one of his sleeve-links and would I let him have mine. I lent them to him. It was snowing. I said "Will you have an umbrella?" and I lent him mine. He said he should like a cab but he had no money. I lent him 5s. He then went away. I never saw my jewellery again till to-day. They are now produced. I sent to Howell and James and to the Bank of London. I never saw him again until to-day.

Signed. ADA WOODING.

REPORT OF THE TRIAL OF JOHN SMITH, AT THE CENTRAL CRIMINAL COURT IN MAY, 1877, CONTAINED IN THE CENTRAL CRIMINAL COURT SESSIONS PAPER, VOL. 86, P. 50.

THIRD COURT.–Thursday, May 10th, 1877.
Before Mr. COMMON SERJEANT.
JOHN SMITH (27). Stealing a pair of earrings, a ring,
and 11s. of Louisa Leonard.
Mr. FULTON *conducted the prosecution, and* Mr. M.
Williams *the defence*

LOUISA LEONARD.–I am married, but living apart
from my husband, at 8, Great College Street. On 4th
April I met the prisoner near Charing Cross. He said
he would write me a letter. I received a letter next
day. He came on the Thursday, when I was moving
from my last residence. My friend Emily Ashton was
with me. He came with me to College Street. He said
he was Lord Willoughby. He came and sat opposite
me in the room, my friend being present, and said he
wished to talk to me very seriously. He had a nice
house at St. John's Wood, and I must give up my
apartments and go there by 8.30 on the following
Saturday, to meet him there to dinner. The address
was Alpha Villa, Abbey Road. He said I was to have a
carriage and pony, and a nice little page and several
servants, and whatever I did I was not to associate
with the servants. He then asked what jewellery I had,
and said "I suppose it is all rubbish?" I said
"Unfortunately it is," and showed him the rings on
my finger. He asked for a plain ring, which appeared
to fit me the best, for a pattern, saying he would send
me some better ones by a Commissionaire from the
Army and Navy Club. He belonged to that club, and
if I wanted any more money I was to apply there for

3

it. I said "You could take the size of the ring without taking the ring." He said he had given a ring to another young lady and had lost it through not taking the size, and he took it. I also had some filagree earrings. He said he admired the patterns, but that they were rubbish, and if I would allow him to take them he would have them made in real gold. He showed me a ring on his finger which had been left him through his ancestors 500 years before Christ. He put the earrings in his pocket. He then asked for pen, ink, and paper, and when it was brought he wrote on it, and I was to give it to Messrs. Howell and James, as he wished me to have good clothing. He also enclosed a cheque in an envelope which he took from his pocket book. He said, "Don't unseal it, because they will think it is not from the Lord" I was to take it to the London Bank, No, 12, Lombard Street. He looked at his watch now and then, and at last said, "It is time you went to the bank, otherwise you won't get this money." After sitting a little while longer, my friend and I went out with him, and in the street he said, "Oh, what a nuisance, I have sent my brougham away. Have you any loose change in your pocket?" I said, "Yes, I have 15s." He said, "Will you let me have it, because you will have plenty when you get to the bank." I said, "You can take 4s. if you want it only for a cab." I handed him my purse, showing him the amount I had. He said, "You may as well let me have it all, because you will have more than enough when you get to the bank; £13 10s. will be more than enough." I objected to his taking the 10s.

He took it and laughed, and added "Don't be afraid." He threw the purse into the road. He then called a cab, and said, "You had better get in this cab and make haste and get to the bank, it is open till 5 o'clock, close the windows"–we got in and drove away, but subsequently changed our four-wheel cab for a hansom because we were not going quick enough–we presented the sealed letter in Lombard Street, the clerks consulted and then said it was a swindle–I did not get any money–I have not since seen my earrings, my ring, or my money–on 19th April, I saw the prisoner in Tottenham Court Road, I was going with my friend to have lunch at the Horseshoe–I said, "There's the Captain"–I said to him, "How are you, you never gave me what you promised"–he said, "You be off, I do not know you, I will give you in custody, who are you?"–I said "I think it is my duty to give you into custody, you have taken my things and it appears to me I shall never see them again"–he walked along quickly and then ran across the road: we followed–I next saw him in custody and charged him–I have no doubt he is the same man.

Cross-examined. When I first met the prisoner he asked me where I lived, I said, "50, Cherrington Street"–I expected better jewellery and earrings–I believed every word he told me.

EMILY ASHTON. I live with the last witness; I recollect the prisoner coming to 8, Great College Street, on a Thursday, in April–he said he was Lord Willoughby–I was present the whole time–he said he had a house at St. John's Wood, and would take my friend to live with him where she was to have servants and a page, and she was to be careful not to associate with the servants–then he said to her, "Let me look at the size of your finger"–I was with her when we saw him in Tottenham Court Road–I am sure the prisoner is the man; I saw him run away–he was given in custody.

JOHN COOK. I live at 24, Fitzroy Place–I saw the prisoner and a crowd on a Friday, in April, running into Gower Street, from Euston Road–I asked the ladies what was the matter and then ran after him–he got into a cab; I got hold of the horse's head–he said, "Drive away, cabby, take no notice of him, hit him with your whip"–the cabman hit me with his whip, but the prisoner finding it was no use jumped out on the other side of the cab–he was taken into custody.

ELISS SPURRELL (Policeman ER 25). I took the prisoner at 5 o'clock, on April 20th, in the Euston Road–he said "Come round a corner in one of the houses; I am perfectly ashamed of this crowd running after me"–Cook then came up and said that he had robbed two ladies–I took the prisoner back to meet the ladies, who told me the charge in his presence–he said nothing.

Cross-examined. He had £4 in gold, and five rings, and an umbrella on him.

JOSIAH WILLEY. I am a partner in the firm of Howell and James, of Regent Street; I do not know the prisoner–I do not know Lord Willoughby.

GEORGE CLARKE. I am a counterman, and live at 16, Abchurch Lane–there is no Bank of London now–there was once, but it did not carry on business at 12, Lombard Street.

WILLIAM REDSTONE (Police Inspector Y). I have searched the Peerage, and can find no Lord Willoughby.

Mr. WILLIAMS *submitted that there was no larceny, the property was entrusted to the prisoner by the prosecutrix, and although it might amount to an obtaining by false pretences, it was no felony.* Mr. FULTON *contended that it was obtained by a trick with the intention to deprive the owner of it, that would amount to a larceny, and* THE COURT *so held.*

GUILTY.

JOHN SMITH (27), was again indicted for stealing one ring and 11s., of Louisa Victoria Howard.

Mr. FULTON *conducted the prosecution; and* Mr. M. WILLIAMS *the defence.*

LOUISA VICTORIA HOWARD. I am single, and live at 4, Limerston Street, Chelsea–on on April 18th, I was getting out of an omnibus in Limerston Street, when I met the prisoner, who asked me the way to Gertrude Street–I told him the way and as he passed my house, I asked him if he would come in–he came in and said he would make an appointment for the next day–I had a letter next morning, and after that the prisoner came–he said he would not tell me who he was, but afterwards said he was Lord Willoughby–I had some flowers in my grate which were rather faded–I said I was going to have them done up by contract–he said "Don't do that, I have a proposal to make to you. I have been keeping a little woman, but have left her three months"–then he said he thought I took his fancy and that he would like me; that he belonged to the Army and Navy Club–I said I knew someone there–he said he knew that–I said, "Why?"–he said he would not tell me–he then said he would allow me £10 a week pin money, and that I should have a pony and carriage, a page and a hack for the park, and that he would pay my debts and buy me dresses–he said he would send me some jewellery next day as I had not sufficient to please him, and a watch and chain, four rings, and £50–he took one of my rings for a pattern–he wanted to take other things, but I would not let him–he gave me a cheque for £13 10s. upon the Bank of London, and wanted change–I gave him 11s.–he also gave me an order to Messrs. Howell and James, for £400 for dresses, I presented the letter. I did not get the dresses. I saw him next at the police station. I have no doubt the prisoner is the man. This ring (*produced*) is mine.

Cross-examined. I believed all he said. I was very pleased. I gave him the ring for him to take the size of my finger; I expected a better wedding ring and a diamond keeper.

WILLIAM REDSTONE (Inspector Officer Y). I took this charge against the prisoner and found the ring produced upon him, with four others–the last witness identified him in the police-court cell–he was placed with other prisoners.

GUILTY–FIVE YEARS' PENAL SERVITUDE.
There was another indictment against the prisoner.

[NOTE.–Facsimiles of the letter and cheque referred to in the evidence of Louisa Victoria Howard are printed at the end of the Appendix. In the letter the witness is addressed as "Mrs. Beaumont."]

–PETITION OF JOHN SMITH, DATED 25TH JUNE, 1879.

25th June, 1879,
Portsmouth Prison.

Name, JOHN SMITH,

Register No. D 523.

To the Right Hon. R. A. Cross, H.M. Principal Secretary of State for the Home Department–

The PETITION of JOHN SMITH, a Prisoner in the Convicts' Prison, HUMBLY SHEWETH–

The most respectfully undersigned was tried at the Old Baily in London for Larceny at the first May Sessions, 1877, and sentenced to five years

P.S.

As his sentence is a very severe one, and he was not sent for trial on the charge for Larceny, but for obtaining money by false pretences, he begs most humbly for a reconsideration of his case and that he may deemed worthy of a remission of part of his sentence.

He begs leave to support this his humble petition by the following extenuating circumstances: firstly, its being his first offence; secondly, the smallness of accusers losses; thirdly, that more than half of his alotted sentence has already expired; and, lastly, his good behaviour during the past term of his imprisonment.

Signed JOHN SMITH.

25th June, 1879.

–DESCRIPTION OF JOHN SMITH AS RELEASED ON LICENCE, 14TH APRIL, 1881.

Date and place of birth 1850, Glasgow.
Height (without shoes) 5 ft. 6 in.
Complexion Dark.
Hair Brown.
Eyes Brown.
Trade or occupation   Labourer.
Married or single   Single.
Distinctive marks or peculiarities:–

Right side.–Scar, bottom lip; scar, upper part of nose and jaw; two vaccination marks; scar, outside arm; mole, armpit.

Left side.–Mole on neck and shoulder; three vaccination marks.

[NOTE.–This description of John Smith was drawn up in Portsmouth Prison, shortly before his release, and was forwarded by the governor of the prison to the police authorities in London on 4th April, 1881.]

1896

*-MEMORANDUM FROM
SUPERINTENDENT NEAME,
CONVICT SUPERVISION OFFICE,
NEW SCOTLAND YARD, TO THE
GOVERNOR, H.M. PRISON,
HOLLOWAY.*

14th January, 1896.

S<small>IR</small>,

I am directed by Mr. Anderson, Assistant Commissioner of Police of the Metropolis, to ask you to be so good as to have the prisoner, Adolf Beck, examined, and forward him a list of his marks, for identification purposes, at your earliest convenience.

Please return enclosed photograph.

I am, &c.,
(Signed)   P. NEAME,
Superintendent.

Indorsement made on the above Memorandum:–

Full description of the prisoner herewith. Photograph also returned.

(Signed) M. CAMPBELL,
Deputy Governor,
15th January, 1896.
Holloway Prison.

–DESCRIPTION OF ADOLF BECK SENT TO THE CONVICT SUPERVISION OFFICE BY THE DEPUTY GOVERNOR OF HOLLOWAY PRISON ON 15TH JANUARY, 1896.

ADOLF BECK

Part bald crown of head.
Scars on forehead and small of back.
Right upper arm long scar.
Mole right side of throat.
Left check, long scar.
Left upper arm, three scars (vaccine marks).

Two blue veins inside left thigh.

Age 48.

Place of birth Norway.

Married or single Single.

Trade or occupation   Mine owner.

Residence   139, Victoria Street, Westminster.

Complexion   Fresh.

Hair   Grey.

Eyes   Blue.

Build   Proportionate.

Shape of face   Oval.

Height 5 feet 5½ inches.

Education   Well.

Religion   P.

–LETTER FROM THE DIRECTORS OF CONVICT PRISONS TO THE TREASURY SOLICITOR, 17TH JANUARY, 1896.

Home Office,
17th January, 1896.

Sir,

I am desired by the Directors of Convict Prisons to return to you the accompanying particulars of Convict D 523 John Smith, and to inform you that the same has been referred to the Governors of Portland and Parkhurst prisons, to which the officers of Portsmouth Prison were transferred, but no officer at either of those prisons can identify him.

I am, &c.,
(Signed) E. G. CLAYTON,
The Solicitor to the Treasury, Secretary
Whitehall, S.W

−THE PARTICULARS OF CONVICT D 523 JOHN SMITH ACCOMPANYING THE ABOVE LETTER.

Description of JOHN SMITH.

Date and place of birth   1845 Glasgow.
Height (without shoes)   5 ft. 6 in.
Complexion   *fresh*.
Hair   Brown.
Eyes   Brown.
Trade or Occupation   Labourer.
Married or Single   Single.
Distinctive marks or peculiarities:−
indent onand between eyebrows

Right Side.−Scar, bottom lip; ^ upper part of nose and jaw; ^ two vaccination marks; scar, outside arm; mole, armpit.

Left Side.−Mole on neck, and shoulder; three vaccination marks.

[NOTE.−The "description" of John Smith supplied on his release by the prison authorities to the police is printed previously. The words and figures printed above in italics are the alterations and additions made on that "description" by the police officer who examined John Smith at Millbank Prison immediately before his release.]

–LETTER FROM MR. T. DUERDIN DUTTON ASKING FOR INSPECTION OF THE RECORD OF JOHN SMITH; POLICE REPORTS THEREON; AND THE REPLY OF DR. (NOW SIR ROBERT) ANDERSON.

6th February 1896.

DEAR SIR,   40, Churton Street, S.W.

R. v. ADOLF BECK.

I am informed by the Prison Commissioners that John Smith alias Vilvoir Weisenfells was convicted at the Central Criminal Court on 7th May, 1877, and sentenced to five years' penal servitude for larceny, that he served portions of his sentence in Pentonville, Wormwood Scrubs, and Portsmouth Convict Prison. From the latter place he was licensed on 14th April 1881 via Millbank to the care of the Royal Society for Assistance of Discharged Prisoners.

It is alleged by the prosecution that this man is Adolf Beck now awaiting trial and whom I am defending. In his interests it is absolutely necessary I

should see the record of the prisoner John Smith and his photo. Will you oblige me with an appointment to inspect documents, and state where I may do so?
Yours truly,
To The Commissioner of Police,
(Signed) T. DUERDIN DUTTON.
Scotland Yard.

Metropolitan Police, King Street Station,
"A" Division,
8th February, 1896.

With reference to the attached, I beg to report that the papers referred to were forwarded to C.O. 13th ultimo, and are now in possession of Inspector Froest.

I therefore respectfully suggest that the inquiry may be forwarded to Superintendent Shore, Central.
(Signed) GEO. WALDOCK,
Local Inspector.
F. BEARD, Superintendent.

SUBJECT:—ADOLPH BECK, in custody.
Metropolitan Police,
Criminal Investigation Department,
New Scotland Yard,
10th February, 1896.

Referring to the attached from Mr. T. Duerdin Dutton, Solicitor, of 40, Churton Street, S.W., who asks to be allowed to see the photographs and records of expiree John Smith, I have to report that these documents are confidential and privileged, therefore they should not be shown to Mr. Dutton.

I have mentioned it to Mr. Sims of the Treasury, who has conducted the prosecution in this case, and he is also of opinion that the documents should not be shown.

(Signed)   BENJ. ALLAN, P.S.

JOHN SHORE, Superintentent.

Convict Supervision Department,
London, S.W.,
10th February, 1896.

SIR,

I HAVE received your letter, but I regret that I cannot comply with your request.

I am, &c.,

To T. Duerdin Dutton, Esq., Solicitor,

(Signed) R. ANDERSON.
40, Churton Street, S.W.

—LETTER FROM MR. T. DUERDIN DUTTON ASKING FOR PRODUCTION OF THE RECORD OF JOHN SMITH AT THE FORTHCOMING TRIAL OF ADOLF BECK; POLICE REPORT THEREON, AND THE REPLY OF DR. (NOW SIR ROBERT) ANDERSON.

40, Churton Street, London, S.W.

20th February 1896.

DEAR SIR,

R. *v.* BECK.

Referring to your letter of the 10th February, in which you say you cannot comply with my request, may I ask you to be good enough to have a complete record of the prisoner "John Smith," convicted at the Central Criminal Court in May 1877, in court at the trial of the above-named prisoner, produced by some person competent to do so, in case the learned Judge trying the case should consider it advisable?

Yours truly,

(Signed) T. DUERDIN DUTTON.

To R. Anderson, Esq.,

Convict Supervision Office,

New Scotland Yard.

Metropolitan Police,

Criminal Investigation Department,

New Scotland Yard,

22nd February, 1896.

Referring to the attached further letter from Mr. T. Duerdin Dutton, who now asks that the "complete record of the prisoner John Smith, convicted at the Central Criminal Court in May 1877," be produced at the trial of Adolf Beck in case the Judge trying the case should consider it advisable, I have to report that the records are not required at court to prove the previous conviction, and I respectfully suggest that they be not produced unless some person is subpœnaed, or the Judge directs that they be produced, and even then objection should be raised against them being shown on the grounds that the records are privileged documents.

Mr. Sims, of the Treasury, who has conducted the prosecution of this case, also suggests that the papers be not produced unless absolutely compelled to do so.

(Signed) BENJAMIN ALLAN, Police Sergeant.

JOHN SHORE, Superintendent.

> Convict Prison Department,
> London, S.W.,
> 22nd February, 1896.

Sir,

I have received your letter, but I regret that I cannot comply with your request.

> I am, &c.,
> (Signed) R. ANDERSON.
> T. Duerdin Dutton, Esq.,

Solicitor,

40, Churton Street, S.W.

–DEPOSITIONS OF WITNESSES TAKEN BEFORE MR. J. SHEIL AT THE WESTMINSTER POLICE COURT ON THE 17TH AND 23RD DECEMBER, 1895, AND THE 9TH, 23RD, AND 30TH JANUARY, 1896.

Metropolitan Police District to wit. The Examination

of OTTILIE MEISSONIER, DAISY GRANT and JOHN WATTS,

taken on Oath this Seventeenth day of December in the Year of Our Lord One thousand Eight hundred and Ninety-five at the Westminster Police Court, in the County of London, and within the Metropolitan Police District before Me, the undersigned, one of the Magistrates of the Police Courts of the Metropolis, sitting at the Police Court aforesaid, in the presence and hearing of Adolph Beck, who is charged this day before Me.

OTTILIE MEISSONIER sworn.

I am single. I live at 36, St. Oswald's Road, Fulham. I met the prisoner on the 26th November. I went to the Westminster Drill Hall to a flower show. In passing through Victoria Street, I met the prisoner. I did not know him before. He passed and turned back and said "Pardon me, are you not Lady Everton or Egerton?" When he saw my face he said "Oh, pardon, I've made a mistake." He asked me where I was going. I said I was going to the Drill Hall to see the Chrysanthemum Show. He told me that he had an estate in Lincolnshire and kept, 10 gardeners. I told him I had just received a box of chrysanthemums. He asked if he could see my flowers. I gave permission for him to come next day between 1 and 2, and he came. My servant let him in; her name is Kate Harvey. He stayed about three-quarters of an hour to an hour. I went to my bedroom to change my dress. He was alone in my sitting-room from three to five minutes.

When I came back he was reading a German news-paper. I brought a watch to show him, the glass was broken. He said it I gave it him he would have it mended, and put a diamond star in its back. He promised to buy me a lot of dresses, and asked for the loan of a ring as he would buy me another.

He asked me to join him in going to the Riviera. He wrote out the paper marked C. He held the pen between his two fingers. He also gave me the cheque D for £40, to pay for the dresses, boots and shoes, bonnets and hats he was going to buy me. I was to make out an invoice. He was going to call on the fol-lowing Wednesday. The envelope marked E is the one he put the cheque in. He wrote the cheque out in my presence, but I think the name was already written. He said he was a cousin of Lord Salisbury's and most of the property round Brompton belonged to him. He said he had £180,000 revenue every year. He asked if I had a watch–I said I had three, and he asked me to show them to him.

The watch with the broken face was a gold watch with a gold chain and a little key attached. I believed what he said and gave it to him. It was worth £10.

I gave him an old-fashioned ring to have one made for me from it. He asked me to give him my diamond ring, it was too small, he would have it made larger. The ring I gave him was worth 30s. He said he would send them back the next day by a porter with one arm, and would send some jewels for me to choose.

Three minutes after he left I missed an antique enamelled watch about the size of a shilling from the table. I showed it to the prisoner and he said he had given his collection of antique watches to South Kensington Museum. The value of my enamelled watch was £10 to £15. I sent my servant after him. The same hour I went in a cab to look for the Union Bank in St. James's Street. I went to the Union Bank in Trafalgar Square, and found he had no account there. I went to Vine Street Station, and gave a description of the person to the police.

I was sent to Jubilee Police Station, Fulham, and gave the description there. Yesterday, at 10 minutes to 5, I saw him standing at the door of a house in Victoria Street. I went to him, looked in his face, and he smiled very sweetly, and I told him, "Sir, I know you." He said: "What do you want from me?" I spoke to him in English. He tried to push away through the gate of the iron railing and go into the street. I followed and said, "Sir, I shall follow you wherever you go." Then he ran over to the other side of Victoria Street, but I followed him. Then he stopped and turned round and said, "You're only a b—dirty bitch," and worse words still. He tried to run away, he more than walked, I could hardly follow him. I gave him into custody just opposite the clock at Victoria Station. I am sure it is the man. I noticed his right cheek was drawn and his left cheek fuller. He took a pocket book out at my house, and wrote in it about dresses, silk stockings and gloves. The pocket book produced is the one. I recognised yesterday that silver match box. I think he had a silver cigarette case. I am sure about the pocket book.

Cross-examined.—I must confess I had never been to Vine Street before. In June, a year ago, I was at a police court to prosecute a servant who had taken about £20 worth of wearing apparel. I was living then where I live now. I have never been charged myself. I decline to say whether I have been married. I have lived 21 months where I am living now. I do not get my living by seeing men. I am a music teacher and I have my own income. I have gone to one family as a teacher four years. Prisoner did not yesterday charge me with annoying and accosting him. It was between two and three on 26th November when I saw him. It might be from a quarter to two to half-past two. I am quite sure about the date and time. I was with him on the 26th about five minutes, and on the 27th about an hour. I saw the prosecutrix in the first case yesterday for the first time. I did not see her again till to-day. I really mean to say that is the book I saw the man with—I have no doubt. I did not have it in my hand on the 27th, I saw some initials on it, but he opened it so quick I didn't see what they were. Both these documents were written in my presence.

On the 26th November, when I met the defendant, it must have been a fairly fine day else I would not have gone out. I have been in this police court as a witness before. A gentleman named Allen, a detective subpœnaed me.

(Signed) OTTILIE MEISSONIER.

DAISY GRANT, sworn.

I live at 44, Circus Road, St. John's Wood. On the

5th July I was living at 3, Wellington Chambers York Street, Westminster. On Thursday the 4th of July I met the prisoner in St. James's Street. I was just returning home. I was with a lady and a little boy. He spoke to me, making a remark about the little boy. I stopped to speak to him and the lady and the little boy went on. He took out his pocket-book and wrote down my name and address. He made an appointment to call the next afternoon. He did call about 4 o'clock. I was at home. He remained about three-quarters of an hour. That was the only visit. He said he would buy me other rings, he was going to Streeter's in Bond Street. He took a small diamond ring to know the size of my finger. He said he would send them by a commissionaire. He was going to give me the things, a list of which I produce. The ring I gave him in order to know the size of my finger, was worth about 30s. He said he would send it back with others by a Commissionaire in half-an-hour. He said I would know the Commissionaire as he had his arm in a sling. I knew there was one who had lost his arm; he is connected with one of the clubs in St. James's. That was why I believed him. I saw him write out a list marked A. He said he was going to give me the things, he was going to take a house for me in Adair Road, St. John's Wood. He told me to buy the things and said where I was to order them. He wrote out the cheque marked B at the same time (cheque dated 5th June). I couldn't say whether it was June or July. He signed the cheque "Wilton." He said he was the Earl Wilton. He did not give me any money besides. He went away and said he would call again on Monday. He sent me out of the room for matches to light a cigarette with, he sent me out twice, once for my photograph and once for a match. I had shown him my marquise ring before he left. It was in a case on the table. About half-an-hour after he left, I missed my ring from the case, which was left behind. I gave him my bracelet—a broad gold bracelet chased on the top, which had been dented. He said he would get the dents taken out.

He did not return or send me anything, and I came to the police court on the Monday I did not see him again till I saw him in custody last evening. I have not got my rings or my bracelet.

The figures in the margin of the list A were different deposits I was to leave at the shops on the goods I bought. The cheque was given to me partly to meet that. I inquired for the Union Bank in St. James's Street, and couldn't find any such bank.

The value of my bracelet was about £3, the diamond ring I gave him as a pattern 30s.; and the marquise ring about £10. I bought the marquise ring off somebody else for £8.

Cross-examined by Mr. DUTTON.

The lady that was with me on the 4th July cannot identify the prisoner. She has told me since that she couldn't identify him. I can't say for certain whether it was in June or July. I believe it was July. It was about five in the afternoon of the 4th July when I first saw the prisoner. It was a fine afternoon. He had on a low hat, a round felt hat—I think it was dark brown. I can't say whether his clothes were light or dark. In my presence he wrote the whole of the cheque B–everything. He put it in an envelope first, and directed the envelope, I think I have the envelope at home among my papers. I did not look at the cheque till after he'd gone. I read it then. I noticed it was on a promissory note. I did not notice it was dated a month earlier. That it was a promissory note and not a cheque from a bank book attracted my attention more than the date. It was given me to order these things on the paper. I was not carrying on a gay life on that day. I certainly spoke to the man when he spoke to me. I was leading a respectable life then. I am living now as a married woman. I decline to say whether I am married. I have been for five years under the keeping of somebody. I was living in my own name as Mrs. Grant. That is my correct name Daisy Grant, prisoner did visit me for a purpose and having no money, gave me that cheque, if you put it that away. The man wrote on the paper B. what is written there, every bit of it in my presence, That is my paper–I took it out of my draw. I identified the prisoner at the station here yesterday, I was sitting with another girl on a form in the station. When I identified the prisoner he was amongst several men. I did not see him before I identified him attempt to enter the room where I was sitting, and then be immediately pushed out by the officer in charge.

Further examined.–I would not have let him have the gold bracelet or the ring if I had not expected he would bring it back to me. I am quite sure he wrote both these things in my presence, I can swear it.

(Signed) DAISY GRANT.

JOHN WATTS, Detective A. Division, sworn.

About 5.45 last night, I saw the prisoner detained at Rochester Row police station on another charge. I told him that he answered the description of a man giving the name of Earl Wilton, who was wanted for stealing jewellery. He said "It's a great mistake. The lady has made a great mistake I never saw her in my life." I then sent for the prosecutrix, Mrs. Grant. The prisoner was placed with six other men. She said "I believe that's the man" touching the prisoner, "if he took his hat off I should know." The prisoner took his hat off, and she said that was the man. He was then charged, and he said he'd never seen the ladies before in his life. I then searched him and found a pocket-book, one £10 Bank of England note, one £5 note, 30s. gold, 2s. 6d. silver, one Army and Navy Stores ticket in the name of A. Beck, several cards and mem-oranda. I then went to 139, Victoria Street, a house let out in chambers, and found that he occupied three rooms there in partnership with a gentleman who is away, I searched all the rooms, but failed to find any cheques or cheque book, or anything relating to the charge.

Cross-examined.–I saw a great number of papers–something to do with mines He has told me that he is connected with some copper mines.

(Signed) JOHN WATTS, P.C., C.I.D.a.

The above depositions of OTTILIE MEISSÔNIER, DAISY GRANT, and JOHN WATTS, were taken and sworn before Me, the undersigned, one of the Magistrates of the Police Courts of the Metropolis at the Police Court aforesaid, on the day and year first above-mentioned.

(Signed) J. SHEIL.

MARCUS BROWNE, sworn.

I am the proprietor of the Covent Garden Hotel. The prisoner was lodging with me down to about September, 1894. I could not get my payment of my bill, and got rid of him and detained his trunk. At that time he owed me about £300. After his arrest in this case I allowed Inspector Froest to make a search of the things I had detained. I was present when they searched. I saw them find some white waistcoats and white spats, and also the book produced (marked No. 8) in manuscript. He had an umbrella with a gold or gilt handle, which he said he thought had been stolen from the hall. My son lost an overcoat about the same time. While he was with me he gave me a pawnticket to mind. It related to a gold watch. I kept it in my cash box. It is produced, marked No. 9.

Cross-examined.–I brought an action against the prisoner and obtained judgment against him. Since then I have had transferred to me certain shares in the Hannan Main Reef. I think my judgment is satisfied. Prisoner always was hard up. I was unable to get my satisfaction of my claim until I attached these shares, which was during the present month. I put my claim in the hands of my solicitors, and they've done what they could to get the money. His clothes were not looking very seedy when he left me, he always dressed well. He lodged at my place nearly six years. I have not had large sums of money from him—I have had some money.

Re-examined.—My claim against prisoner was not for board and lodging only. I had advanced him money—about £1,400; on one occasion I lent him money to go to Norway to assist him in his mines and also to assist him in bringing out the companies in connection with the copper mines he was supposed to have in Norway.

(Signed) M. A. S. BROWNE.

GODFREY CHETWYND, sworn.

I live at 13A, Cockspur Street. Financial broker. In June, 1894, the prisoner called on me and discussed some business with me with respect to a copper mine. I afterwards had some business transactions with him. In the course of these transactions I had to write to him from time to time. I had replies to my letters. The three produced, 10, 11, 12, are three of them. They are addressed from the Buckingham Hotel, Buckingham Street, Strand. I paid his weekly bill while he was there, occasionally I handed him the money. My office is at 13A, Cockspur Street. I do not reside there.

(Signed.) GODFREY J. B. CHETWYND

THOMAS HENRY GURRIN, sworn.

My address is 59, Holborn Viaduct. I am an expert in handwriting. I have followed that occupation for about 11 years, and given evidence in a large number of cases. I have had submitted to me for examination the exhibits in this case, particularly the cheques produced by the various female witnesses, the lists of dresses and the envelopes in which the cheques were contained, and also the letter and envelope upon the Grand Hotel notepaper. I have carefully examined these exhibits. In my opinion they are all in the handwriting of one person. I can if necessary give my reasons for that opinion. I have also examined the book containing address marked No. 1, and the five documents written in pencil marked 2, 3, 4, 5 and 6, and the letter and envelope marked No. 7. I have also examined the writing in the manuscript book marked No. 8, and the letters produced by Mr. Chetwynd marked 10, 11 and 12. In my opinion these documents are undoubtedly in the handwriting of one person. I have compared the two sets, the set marked with the letters and the set marked with numbers, and I have formed the opinion they were all written by one person, one set of course being disguised. I should describe the general character of the hand as Scandinavian. In the exhibits marked with letters, I find more than one style of writing. There are two styles of writing on the bills, cheques and lists. One is either vertical or sloping to the left–back handed, and the other has the natural slope to the right. The writing sloping to the left or written vertically, was written under the control of the arm rather than the muscles of the fingers and thumb. It appears to have been written without any effort—with ease.

The other writing appears to me to be a laboured writing in which the pen was immediately under the control of the muscles of the thumb and fingers. I have carefully examined these documents and made tracings of them, and can give my reasons for my opinions if they are wanted.

Cross-examined. I mean by Scandinavian a handwriting written by persons in those Northern countries, Norway, Denmark, Sweden, Finland. The writing which I inspected is mostly of that type. Some of the writing written with the fore-arm on account of being rapidly written does not show these characteristics. I am referring to the class of writing that you find in the signatures of the cheques and also on the envelopes enclosing the cheques. I don't say that that is not of the Scandinavian type. I say that owing to its having been written rapidly I cannot detect the Scandinavian characteristics, in fact some of it is illegible. The Exhibits that are of the Scandinavian type of writing are, first the pocket book (No. 1), next the other book (No. 8) the documents 2, 3, 4, 5, 6, and 7, 10, 11, and 12, the handwriting in the body of most of the cheques speaking roughly. That fairly conveys my view. The remaining documents and the remaining portions of the cheques are in the Scandinavian type of writing, but they are disguised. When I say there are two styles of writing I mean one is natural and the other is feigned or disguised. On some of the documents we have both styles. Those marked 1, 2, and 3, and so on are of the first kind. With regard to the cheques there are two writings, both of which are in my opinion disguised, but, with reference to a portion the style is much more like the natural handwriting because written at the same slope. I have no objection to put in my report. It is numbered 13. The whole of the documents put to me in this case I have found to be undoubtedly in the same handwriting. You don't include that book No. 1. In that I found two distinct handwritings.

Signed. T. H. GURRIN.

ELISS SPURREL, sworn.

I live now at 19, Broadley Terrace, Marylebone. I am pensioned from the Metropolitan Police.

In 1877 I was in the Metropolitan Police E Reserve stationed at Hunter Street. On the 7th of May, 1877, I was present at the Central Criminal Court when the prisoner in the name of John Smith was convicted of felony, stealing ear rings and a ring and 11s. in money, the property of Louisa Leonard, and sentenced to five years' penal servitude. I produce the certificate of that conviction marked Y. The prisoner is the man.

Cross-examined. There is no doubt whatever he is the man. I know what's at stake on my answer, and I may say without doubt he's the man. I took him in custody. I don't know where he was living. He was taken in custody at Euston Road. I could not find his address. The prisoner then represented himself as Lord Willoughby. I was unable to find out where he'd been living. There was nothing found out about him. I did not find out how long he had been in London before he was arrested. I only found out that he'd been to these different addresses in the 17 similar cases on that occasion. Smith did not give any account of himself. When he was charged he gave the name of Lord Willoughby. When he came before the Magistrate he gave the name of Smith and refused his address. Inspector Redstone who took the charge also took part in the inquiry.

(Signed) ELISS SPURRELL.

The above depositions of FRANK COOPER, MINNIE LEWIS, EVELYN EMILIE MILLER, MARCUS BROWN, GODFREY CHETWYND, THOMAS HENRY GURRIN, and ELISS SPURRELL were taken and sworn before Me, the undersigned, one of the Magistrates of the Police Courts of the Metropolis, at the Police Court, afore-said, on the day and year first above mentioned.

(Signed) J. SHEIL.

STATEMENT OF THE ACCUSED.–ADOLF BECK (hereinafter called the ACCUSED) stands charged before the undersigned one of the Magistrates of the Police Courts of Metropolis sitting at the Westminster Police Court, in the Metropolitan Police District, this 30th day of January in year of our Lord One Thousand Eight Hundred and Ninety-six as hereinbefore set forth, and the said charge being read to the said ACCUSED, and the said WIT-NESSES for the Prosecution being severally examined in the presence of the said ACCUSED, the said ACCUSED is now addressed by Me as follows:–

"Having heard the evidence do you wish to say anything in answer to the charge? You are not obliged to say anything unless you desire to do so, but whatever you say will be taken down in writing and may be given in evidence against you upon your trial, and if you desire to call any witness, you can now do so."

Whereupon the said ACCUSED saith as follows:–
"No."

Taken before me at the police court aforesaid, on the day and year above-mentioned.

(Signed) J. SHEIL.

–EXTRACT FROM THE REPORT OF MR. T. H. GURRIN, 29TH JANUARY, 1896.

I should also add that in accordance with instructions received from the Treasury I have examined at the Old Bailey the exhibits in the case of Smith, alias Willoughby, of 1877, and, having compared the exhibits therein with the bills and cheques in this case I am perfectly satisfied that they are all in the self-same handwriting–the disguise then adopted is the same as that now adopted, and the exhibits in that case must, in my opinion, have been written by the person who has written the bills and cheques in this case."

Extracts from the Record of theCentral Criminal
Court Sessions commencing the 24th February, 1896.

THE QUEEN v. ADOLF BECK.

Brief for the Prosecution.

The prisoner who describes himself as a company
promoter and concession vendor but who is really a
foreign adventurer and ex-convict, is charged with
robbing and defrauding a large number of the better
class of gay women.

From the proofs it will be seen that the story told by the prisoner was as nearly as possible identical in every case, and that the lists of dresses, most of which are produced, are also identical; this fact is of importance when it is stated that the defence is that the prisoner is unable to write English with any degree of ease; because if this was the case it will be seen that the prisoner had simply to remember a set form of words and to write the same characters on every occasion; thus as he used the same form of letters his task would present no difficulties to one who was ignorant of or unskilled in the use of the English language.

Beyond this, however, and so long ago as 1877, the prisoner was convicted of a precisely similar offence, giving on that occasion the name of Lord de Willoughby (otherwise John Smith), and the exhibits in that case, which have luckily been preserved, are found to be in precisely the same writing and the same language as the documents in the present prosecution.

In view of this fact it is scarcely necessary to point out how weak is a defence based upon the prisoner's alleged incapacity to speak or write the English language with ease.

The general defence, it should be said, is an alibi. All along it has been contended by Mr. Dutton, who has fought the case very fiercely, that the prisoner is the victim of some huge mistake; that he has never seen any of the women, never wrote any of the cheques and was carrying on a respectable business as a company promoter, at the time when, as the various witnesses allege, he was robbing and swindling them.

As to this it should be said that not a single witness has been called to account for the prisoner's time or doings on any one of the many occasions spoken to by the witnesses; and, what is more remarkable, that although the exhibits of a great number of them, were examined by Mr. Inglis, an expert, on his behalf, this gentleman was not called at the police court, and up to the present no intimation has been received that it is intended to use him as a witness at the trial. No doubt this is in consequence of his having (as is the fact) stated that his opinion would be of no assistance whatever to the defence.

As against the suggestion that the identification is a mistake, it should be pointed out that the prisoner is identified by no less than 11 different women, all of them strangers to each other, and that the writing of the various exhibits is proved by Mr. Gurrin to be in the handwriting of the prisoner.

With reference to the previous conviction, that is proved by ex-Police Constable Spurrell, who took the prisoner into custody. If necessary ex-Inspector Redstone, who had charge of the case before the Magistrate and at the Central Criminal Court, is also prepared to identify him. The case is reported in the Sessions Papers for May, 1877, and a copy of the depositions and exhibits is sent here for reference.

Altogether there were seventeen charges precisely similar to those now under investigation, but only three were proceeded with. The prisoner was prosecuted by Mr. Forrest Fulton and defended by Mr. Montagu Williams. The sentence was five years' penal servitude.

The exhibits in the case have been examined by Mr. Gurrin, who says, as is obviously the fact, that they are in the same handwriting as the documents in the present case, and they will be in Court for reference if necessary.

Evidence for the Prosecution

ETHEL ANNIE TOWNSEND I am a widow. In March 1895, I was living in a flat in Shaftsbury Avenue. On March 6th, I was walking with my little daughter in Piccadilly about 1.15 p.m., when the prisoner asked me if I was Lady somebody (I do nor remember the name he used); I said I was not, unfortunately. He asked me then where I was living, and if I knew Lord Aberdeen. I said I did but I knew his brother better. I thought by that I knew the prisoner, and had met him at dinner somewhere. He said he had just come back from Canada, and that he had been staying with the Earl of Aberdeen, and should like to talk to me about him, and he asked if he might call. I said "Yes" and gave him my card; he did not say who he was. He kept his handkerchief to the left side of his face; and when he came to my flat he did the same thing. He said he would calll at four the next afternoon. He came at about 3.40; my sister let him in, and he came into the drawing room. He did not keep his handkerchief to his face the whole time, only while my sister was letting him in, and part of the time he was with me; he stayed about 20 minutes. He said he was Lord Winton de Willoughby . He asked why I lived alone in a flat. I said I had an income and wished to do so. He asked me if I would prefer to live in St. John's Wood. I said I should very much like it, but I should want to know something about him first. He said he had a little house there, with, I think twelve servants. It was standing empty at the time, with the exception of the servants; that he had a carriage and pair, and a wine cellar, and everything requisite, but no lady in possession, and that he would call and take me to see it. He said he did not think I was dressed sufficiently well and he wished to buy me some new clothes and diamonds and he wished me to write a list of what I wanted. I wrote the list, which he dictated to me; he said I was to get some of the things at Redfern's. I destroyed the list about two days, finding he did not return. He said he would give me £150 to go on with. I saw him write out a cheque for £120; he put it in an envelope and sealed it. He said he would send me some jewellery from Streeter's, and asked me for a ring for the size of my finger; he promised me a few diamond rings. I gave him the only ring I had on at the time; my wedding ring , for the size. He said the ring would come back by a commissionaire with one arm. He said he would make an appointment with me as to the house in St. John's Wood in two or three days time. He looked at a thick gold curb bracelet I had on and said he thought it ought to be set with a diamond in the padlock. I gave it to him. He also took my sister's bracelet from the table to have some dents knocked out. He took an ostrich feather fan, that had cost fourteen guineas to have it mounted with turquoise, and a pair of elephant's tusks (I have a similar pair worth fifty guineas, to have mounted as an inkstand, and a hand painted porcelain photograph of myself. I left the room to get some tea. Two or three hours after he had gone I missed some tigers' claws and the teeth of an animal mounted in silver on my monogram, they had all been in the room in which he had been sitting. I valued the property he got from me at £180 but it was worth more. Next day I took his cheque to the bank at Balham. I was asked to put my name and address on it; the bank kept it, and it was dishonoured. Two days afterwards I communicated with the police at Vine Street and gave a description of the prisoner and the name he had given me. I did not see the prisoner again till I saw him at the police court on December 23rd. The police came for me and I went and saw thirteen men in the yard of Westminster Police Court, and I at once recognised the prisoner. Immediately I heard him speak I was doubtful, as he spoke in my flat in a Yankee twang, and in the police court in a foreign accent; I thought it was Swiss. His hands, hair and feet are the same as I noticed before. He is the same man.

FREDERICK EDWARDS (419 A).–About 5 p.m., on December 16th, I was on duty in Victoria Street, outside the Royal Standard Music Hall, near Victoria Station, when the prisoner and Madame Meissonier came up to me. The prisoner wanted to know what he could do with the woman, as she kept following him about and annoying him, he said. I told him I must hear what she had to say. She said she wished to give him into custody for stealing two watches and a gold ring from her house a fortnight before. I asked her if she would take the responsibility of charging him herself. She said she would. The prisoner said he did not know her, and had never seen her before in his life, I told him he would have to go to the station. He said he was quite willing to do so, and he at once went with me. The charge was read over to him there; he said he did not know the woman. Harvey came to the station and picked him out from others.

Cross-examined.–I did not ask him for his name and address in the street. At the station he was asked for it, and he gave it as Adolf Beck, 139, Victoria Street. He was living there at the time. He had on an overcoat and high hat. I did not search him. I did not notice his boots. The inspector on duty arranged the identifications: I was there at the time. About eight or nine men were got from the street, and some from the adjoining shops; most of them were well dressed I think. Their ages ranged from 30 upwards, I should say. Two, in addition to the prisoner, had grey hair. I think they were about the prisoner's height. One came from the shop opposite. He was not much like the prisoner in appearance; except that his hair was grey, I do not think there was any similarity in appearance. The other, who was about the prisoner's height, and with grey hair, happened to be walking past.

GODFREY CHETWYND.–I am a financial broker, at

13A, Cockspur Street. In June, 1894, the prisoner called with reference to some company in connexion with a copper mine he owns in Norway. After that I wrote to and received letters from him upon that and other business matters. These are three I received from him. He was then living at the Buckingham Hotel, Buckingham Street, Strand. I had business relations and communications with him up to about December 22nd or 23rd. 1894; they were renewed afterwards. The final date I saw him was April or May, 1895. I cannot say where he was living then without referring to my books. While he was visiting my office I believe my clerk wrote some letters for him; I only know that by hearsay. The clerk is not in my employment now, and is not here.

Cross-examined.–I believe my clerk did some correspondence for him, but I cannot say what. I saw the prisoner on and off from June 1894 to the end of the year, and again once or twice in 1895. I never saw him with a gold watch and chain; I have heard him speak of having owned one. If he carried a watch it never attracted my attention. I don't remember seeing any jewellery about him. In December, 1894, and the beginning of January, 1895, he generally wore an overcoat that I gave him; one I had worn myself. He returned it soon after the new year, 1895, or about Christmas 1894. The beginning of 1895 was exceeding cold, and he wore a fur coat then. I knew he had a fur coat before I gave him mine. I gave him mine because he said he had no coat suitable for the season; the fur coat was too warm. I did not see him wearing a fur coat. I did not see him for some time after that. He sometimes wore a double-breasted black jacket when he came to see me. I never saw him wear a white waistcoat or a waistcoat with a white lining. I never noticed him wearing patent button boots, or white or black spats. I remember his saying his frock-coat had been turned at a tailor's. The overcoat I lent him was dark grey; it might have been taken for black. It had no velvet collar; it was perfectly plain. I should not think it could be mistaken for blue. I have no recollection of seeing him wear any other overcoat than the one I lent him and the fur coat. He never wore a covert coat to my knowledge.

Re-examined.–Some time this year I was asked whether I could say if the prisoner was shabbily dressed at the time he came to my office. I have no distinct recollection of the way he used to dress from day to day. I don't remember having ever seen him wear spats; I think the frock-coat he wore had silk facings, I don't remember; but one would be apt to notice a frock-coat that had not; I should gather he meant the coat had been turned inside out. In 1894 I had a good many interviews with him, he borrowed a good deal of money in small amounts for daily expenses, 10s. and 5s. I also paid his weekly hotel bill occasionally.

JOHN WATTS (Constable A).–On December 16th I was at Rochester Row Police Station shortly after the prisoner was brought in, I told him he answered the description of a man giving the name of Earl Wilton, who was wanted for stealing jewellery, he said, "It is a great mistake." I sent for Miss Grant, who had given a description, she came, the prisoner was placed, with six other men, in the charge-room. She looked at the men and pointed to the prisoner, and said, "I believe that is the man; if he will take his hat off I shall know." All the men took their hats off, and then she said, "That is the man." I charged him with stealing the property of Daisy Grant. He said, "It is a great mistake; I have never seen the ladies before in my life," referring to Madame Meissonier and Daisy Grant. He was charged with stealing from both of them. I searched him, and found on him this brown leather pocket-book, with silver mounting, and the initials "A. B.," a £10 note, a £5 note, an Army and Navy Stores ticket, 30s. in gold, 2s. 6d. silver, a knife, a tobacco box, and some visiting cards with the name of "A. Beck, 139, Victoria Street." He gave his name and address before I found the cards. I went to 139, Victoria Street about twenty minutes after he was charged. I found he had been in occupation of three rooms which were sublet to him. There was a porter in charge of the whole building, but no one in charge of this suite of rooms. I had the keys. I found in the rooms about six or seven suits of clothes, a black frock-coat, two ordinary overcoats, besides the one produced, which he was wearing when arrested. I did not take very particular notice of them. I did not bring any of the clothing away. I noticed a new pair of patent boots in paper, they had never been worn. On December 18th I made a further search with another constable. I found this indexed address-book. He had a bedroom, sitting-room, and a small anteroom–a friend of the prisoner had previously occupied them, and had sublet them to prisoner, who was the only occupant at that time. I found these documents, one of which is a letter addressed to a lady, but apparently not sent, the others are memoranda of addresses of ladies apparently. The lettered address-book contains the names of business people apparently, most, foreigners; I cannot find the names and addresses of any women in it. I also found eight or nine pawntickets relating to jewellery; I left them behind; they were dated 1890 and 1891. I also saw printed papers apparently relating to a mine or mines, in Norwegian or some foreign language, I could read the title at the top. I don't know that has since become of the things I left behind in the rooms: the clothes were removed two or three days afterwards, I believe, after the prisoner was in custody. I called again, and found they were gone.

Cross-examined.–When I got to the station I found the prisoner detained on Madame Meissonier's charge; he was not charged, he had given his address, I searched him after he was charged, some time after he was at the station. Miss Grant had to be fetched from St. John's Wood. He was wearing a small link-pattern gold watch chain and a dark gun-metal watch; he also had a small silver match-box; no other articles of jewellery, he wore an overcoat and a high silk hat; his other clothes were as they are now, he had this umbrella with a silver top; I am not sure about his boots. I found no promissory note or bill of exchange form. I found no entry in the pocket, book of the name and address of any of these women, or of any particulars of clothing I should say about fifteen or sixteen women have seen him between the time of his arrest and his committal. I should say there had been about twenty complaints from different parts of the Metropolis of the same kind of thing complained of in the present case, the dates would be kept; I do not know them; Sergeant Briggs and Cracknell would have the dates when the complaints were made; they were here this morning. I arranged the identification in the first case, when the prisoner was detained at Rochester Row Police Station; on the next occasion Inspector Waldock arranged it. I looked through all the papers at the prisoner's address; I made very careful search to try and find some cheques. I found no paper with the name and address of any woman, no cheque, and no bill form. I have been in this case throughout, no single article of property belonging to any of the ten different women has been traced to the prisoner's possession. Whenever a complaint of such a thing as this is made, we take the date of when it is alleged to have occurred, and a description; we are always very careful about the date. It was a pair of new patent shoes I found at his address, they had never been worn; there was a dress suit there.

Re-examined.–The fifteen or sixteen women who saw him at the police station include the ten who have sworn to him here, the other five or six did not identify him: one woman was not sure, she would not swear to him. The five or six women who are not here saw him under the same circumstances as the others, three failed to identify him: they said they could not see the man there. Another of them came into the charge-room while he was in the dock being charged, and she said she did not think he was the man. Another of them afterwards said she thought he was the man. All of them but one had lodged complaints, I believe. I believe I can get the dates on which the five or six women complained. I ascertained that the prisoner had been living at Victoria Street for about three months: he went there about September 6th.

JAMES NORRIS SUTTON.–I am cashier at the Union Bank of London, 66, Charing Cross. We have no branch in St. James's Street or Belgrave Mansions. We have no customer named A. Winton, Lord Wilton or Lord Willoughby de Winton, or any name of that kind. During the year 1895, a number of cheques, most of them drawn on bills of exchange forms, were presented by different ladies, and with this signature, which I cannot decipher. I knew nothing of the drawer, and had no money to meet the cheques, and I dishonoured and returned them. These exhibits were so presented for payment at our bank and dishonoured.

Cross-examined.–All of them were on promissory note forms. There were 15 or 20 altogether, and I should think during between 18 months and two years. We kept no record, because they were not drawn on our bank. They were all the same kind of document; as soon as I saw one I recognised it. I don't remember keeping any.

WILLIAM JOHN WEY.–I am cashier in the Balham

branch of the London and South Western Bank. On November 10th, 1894, Mrs. Gardiner opened an account with our branch. I issued to her a book of 25 cheques, Nos. A 482776 to 800. On January 4th, 1895, I received notice from her to stop cheques in that book, Nos. from 482791 to 800. She gave a reason for that. Subsequently seven of those cheques were presented. Exhibits J, L, and V, were three of them. They were all signed like those produced, with the signature "Wilton," that is the name they were put down to. In some cases I got the ladies who presented them to endorse them. That was on the instruction of the police. I gave them up to the police. I have not seen Mrs. Gardiner since.

Cross-examined.—I could not give you the dates the cheques were presented. We do not keep dates unless the cheque comes into the accounts. We detained the cheques in every case. I produced seven to the police. I had received notice from our customer they had been stolen (*the cheques produced*).

Re-examined.—The dates run from January 28th to March 7th, 1895.

MARCUS BROWNE—I am the proprietor of the Covent Garden Hotel. The prisoner lived there for some years down to within the last two years. I could not tell you the date without referring to my books, and I do not carry them in my pocket. You should have given me notice to look. It might be September 1894. I have so many people to see, I cannot recollect every individual who comes to the hotel, the time he leaves, and so on. I cannot tell whether it was September or

January. I am in a criminal court, and I have nothing to do with a criminal case; you can apply to my solicitors in the City and they will tell you, may be. The prisoner lived at my house about six years; he left because he had not paid his bill, and I said I could not keep him any longer. Apply to my solicitor: the bill is my business, not yours. That has nothing to do with a criminal court whether he owes me money or whether he does not; go to my solicitor, you have my solicitor to go to. Am I obliged to answer what was owing to me? He owed me £300 as far as the hotel bill went, and he owed me hundreds in money lent to him. I could not tell you the amount; you must apply to my solicitors, they have got all the information; they have got all my papers. (*The witness was here cautioned not to withhold information.*) I am quite aware you have power to commit me. The amount is between £1,300 and £1,400. A lot of the prisoner's boxes are at the hotel. He left them. Inspector Froest has searched them. I believe he had a watch; I do not recollect the kind of watch. He gave me a pawnticket for a gold watch, which I gave to Inspector Froest. He always dressed very nicely, and behaved very gentlemanly, and never brought any persons into the house. I should not notice with 20 or 30 in the house whether any individual wore spats. I have not said at the police court I did notice the prisoner wore white spats. I cannot recollect whether he did.

Cross-examined–Who is the prisoner's solicitor?–I do not recollect seeing him I saw Mr. Froest. I did not recollect a gentleman calling at the hotel to see the prisoner's things. I did refuse to allow the prisoner's solicitor to see anything in the place, you have got the letter no doubt; because I did not know whether I was doing right or wrong. I have heard nothing from him since. As to an action against the prisoner, that has to do with a civil court and with my solicitor. I was not winking at the prisoner; he is no friend of mine. I brought an action against him. I believe my solicitors have the judgment. I am satisfied if my solicitors are.

FRANK FROEST (Detective Inspector).–I searched the prisoner's box at the Covent Garden Hotel–I found a pair of white spats, a pair of brown spats, half-a-dozen white waistcoats, a quantity of underclothing, an opera hat, a wedding ring, a few photographs of ladies, and views of Norway and Sweden, and a large quantity of correspondence relating to business.

Cross-examined.–I understood Beck had been staying at the hotel up to September two years ago; that his things were detained. I have seen Mr. Browne calmer than he was here. Afterwards he was living at the Buckingham Hotel, Strand. I went there I did not go to Victoria Street. I did not take charge of the case till after January 3rd. (*A white waistcoat was here produced.*) That is a specimen of the waistcoats; they were all of this class. There was some silk underclothing; old things. I have made inquiries about Mrs. Gardiner. She has been convicted of uttering bad cheques, and passing herself off as a person of distinction. A warrant was out against her for assault. I have not seen her. She led a loose and fraudulent life. She lived once at Balham. She was charged, with others, at Westminster, and after several remands discharged.

Re-examined.–The charge of assault was withdrawn by her landlady. I have made every effort to find her whereabouts to subpœna her as a witness here. I was not in charge of this case until the third remand. I did not sanction the prisoner's clothes being left at his lodgings. I would not have left them.

THOMAS HENRY GURRIN.–I am an expert in handwriting, at 59, Holborn Viaduct. I have had many years' experience. I have examined the cheques and promissory note forms produced; also this manuscript book. (*Mr. Froest identified the book as the one he found at the Covent Garden Hotel, and which purported to be a report of the Galapagos Mine.*) I have also examined the three letters which Chetwynd has sworn to be the prisoner's writing. They are written to Chetwynd. They are all in the same writing. There are two handwritings in the book. I do not include all the handwritings there. I include the writing in the address book produced. The prisoner's writing is in different hands. I prepared the report produced, giving my reasons, and with *facsimiles* showing similarities. The cheques and lists are not written in the prisoner's ordinary hand. Two forms of disguise have been adopted. One is a back-handed or vertical scribble. That occurs in the signatures, the list of addresses, and on the envelopes. The other disguise is an ordinary hand, more resembling his writing in the books but written large and more distorted.

Cross-examined.–The lists of dresses are written with freedom. The control of the fingers is not exercised; it is written with the arm. A man who habituated his hand to it would acquire facility. List "A" is a medium writing between the two disguises. The photographs are very much reduced. Part of "A" was dashed off. I mean "Redfern's" at the top and "Gobb, Baker Street," and one or two other instances, as to which little control was exercised. I do not suggest he held his pen differently. (*The witness pointed out the similarities in the documents.*)

Mr. Gill was proceeding to cross-examine as to the handwriting of certain other documents, exhibits in the case of a man Smith, tried in 1877. Mr. Avory objected to the witness being cross-examined with a view of raising the question whether the prisoner was the person convicted in 1877 of an offence similar to that charged in the indictment; that was a collateral issue, and should not be inquired into until after the jury had returned their verdict, lest it should afterwards be said that the prisoner had been improperly convicted. Mr. Gill urged that the question was directly in issue, and that he was entitled to raise it, as his case on behalf of the prisoner was that the man who was convicted in 1877 was the man who had been committing these frauds, and that the prisoner had been mistaken for that man. He desired to show, by cross-examination, that the writing of the man convicted in 1877 was the same as that of the exhibits in the present case.

Mr. Gurrin stated that the exhibits in the case of Smith were examined by him some time after he had made his report; there was a reference in his report, produced at the police court, to the exhibits in that case. Mr. Gill further con-

tended that upon the question of the value of the witness's opinion he was entitled to have all the documents produced which had been submitted to him. Mr. Avory objected to the witness being asked whether those exhibits were in the same writing as the lists in the present case. The Common Sergeant ruled that the question whether the prisoner was or was not the man convicted in 1877 was not admissible, upon the ground that it related to another and distinct issue, and one calculated to mislead the jury. If witnesses were called to character, Mr. Avory might cross-examine them as to the prisoner's previous character; or he might choose not to have the issue confused by the introduction of that matter).

Re-examined.–The writing is that of a foreigner; it is the Scandinavian type, which would include Norway, as distinguished from the German or the French type but not far from the German type; it is distinct from the English type, which, as a rule, is after the Italian. (*The witness further pointed out the similarities in the documents.*

WILLIAM PARSONS.–I am a warder of Her Majesty's Prison, Holloway. I made a special examination of the prisoner about three weeks after he was received in custody. I found a mark on the right side of his throat, I could not describe it as a scar. I also found a mole on the right side of it.

Cross-examined.–It is not the mark from a double chin. The examination of prisoners is usual, as a record for future use, so that a man can be afterwards identified. Photographs are also taken. I have not photographed him as my prisoner. I was told to make the special examination seven or eight weeks ago. I did not know I was to become a witness till a warder spoke to me this morning. I have not been shown a record of a man sentenced to five years' penal servitude, named Smith.

ALBERT ERNEST LAMB.–I am a clerk in the Solicitor's Department of the Treasury-I was present when the exhibits in this case were produced at the Treasury for inspection by Mr. Inglis, an expert in handwriting. He attended on behalf of the defendant on January 8th.

Cross-examined.–I was partly cognisant of the conduct of this case. I cannot speak personally of Mr. Dutton's application for the dates of offences, or of all that went on in the office.

JOHN WATTS (Detective A.) *Re-examined*–I produce dates of complaints in two cases; one of May 9th, reported on May 10th, 1895, at New Scotland Yard; the other is of April 16th. The offence complained of was on April 13th, 1895. The officer took the report, and referred to another complaint by Miss Minnie Lewis, but it does not give a description of the prisoner. Two others complained, but gave no information, they came to the police court amongst other witnesses, but failed to identify.

Cross-examined.–In two cases the witnesses were sent for in consequence of information the police had possession of, to identify the prisoner. They both gave descriptions.

Evidence for the defence

HENRY HERMAN ELLIS.—I am one of the firm of J. and H. Ellis, tailors, of Farringdon Street. I have known the prisoner since the end of February or the beginning of March, 1895. He came on a matter of business with a lady. He had a fur coat and under it a serge suit. His first order for clothes was in March. he told me he would take the suit away as soon as he could pay for it. I had said, "Our terms are cash." When he took them away he was wearing the same serge suit, a double-breasted reefer. The price of the suit was £3 10s. He then gave orders for a lot of goods. His serge suit was rather shabby. He bought some white waistcoats the 14th or 15th of last September. Then he sent all his wardrobe for me to clean, as he said he was going to survey some mining property in Norway. There were four suits and an extra pair of trousers. There were no white waistcoats. The clothes were very shabby. I have never seen the prisoner wear a white waistcoat, only those I made in September.

Cross-examined.—I saw him in November, and we made him several other things. I saw him the end of September. He told me when he returned that he went to Norway in October. I returned him his clothes in September to take with him. I pressed them up. He paid me. The cleaners sent two or three back as not worth cleaning. I saw him again about the end of November, when he gave me a further order. They were four dress vests that he ordered on September 14th. There was no frock-coat sent to be done up. We made him a frock-coat about June or July; it had silk facings. I cannot recollect where I sent it without referring to my books. In February or March he lived at Buckingham Hotel, Strand.

Re-examined.–I had made him a dress suit, and for that I made the waistcoats. I never made him a white lining to wear inside a black waistcoat.

ANNIE SMITH.–I am chambermaid at the Buckingham Hotel, Strand. Beck was there when I went in, I think, February, 1894. Beck stayed there till last September. I saw his clothes. He had his things washed there. I never saw him with a gold watch. I saw him with a black one, like that produced and a gold chain. I never saw jewellery in his rooms. Up to May or June, 1895, he was rather shabby, when he began to brighten up. After that he had good clothes. I never saw him wear a white waistcoat. I never sent any to the wash. I never saw him wear white spats. He had a black overcoat lined with fur; he wore it a good deal. I looked after his room. I was in it every day. I have never seen elephant's tusks or a mandoline there. I have seen him writing; letters I believe. He wrote very badly and slowly.

Cross-examined.–I have been at the hotel two years. (*Mr. Froest explained he had not been allowed to see the hotel books to get the dates.*) Beck had a bedroom, and the use of the coffee room and drawing room. He had no sitting-room of his own. He wrote in his bedroom in the evening as a rule. He was generally out during the day. He never wrote to me. He sent me a note. It was a letter of half-a-dozen words. I had forgotten that. I have not got the letter. It was last August. In the letter he hoped I was enjoying my holiday, and he would be pleased to see me back. He did not go till September. I think he went to Victoria Street. He did not tell me the number. He took a large portmanteau and a black box. I did not help him pack. I could not help noticing his clothes; they were hanging in the room. There were a good many of them. He had the portmanteau when I went there; the box came later, about June, I think. He had a dark blue overcoat with a velvet collar, and an old frock-coat with silk facings, but he very seldom wore it. He had it all the time he was there. His watch used to lie on his dressing-table in the morning. I believe he had a pearl pin, but I did not much notice. He had a little pin of some kind. It looked like pearl. He wore spats, but they were dark blue or black always. Only one pair that I saw, He wore them last winter; I don't know about "always"; he was wearing them when I went there.

Re-examined.—I brushed his clothes. I do not know whether his coat had been turned. I heard of his being in custody. Several officers have been to see me; about four, I think; two wrote down what I said, one I know did. I think Mr. Froest.

CHARLES GEORGE KISTNER.—I am a clerk to Messrs, Jenkins, Baker and Co., Solicitors, St. Michael's House, Cornhill, About the middle of January, 1895, Beck came to the office practically every day, sometimes before I got there at ten. He was there sometimes all day. He was introducing a mine, the Hannen's Reef. Then he went to Ward and Chandler's. He was paid considerable sums of money in respect of the mine. One cheque in September, 1895, was for £282; one in October for £100, and he had 3,500 shares allotted him. His dress was "medium" the early part of the year, but afterwards he was better dressed. I never saw him with a massive gold chain, gold watch, nor pearl pin. He had an oxidised watch. I should say this is the one he was wearing. I did not see a chain; he used to take it out of his ticket pocket. I have seen him writing. His writing was laboured. The longest time he has been at the office has been from 9 45 a.m. till 7 or 8 p.m. This was about March. I drafted him a letter which he took away.

Cross-examined.–I was told he was a Norwegian. He spoke Spanish. He spoke with a foreign accent. His dress improved towards June or July. He wore a high hat. He had a fur-lined overcoat; I never saw him in any other overcoat. I could not see what he wrote. I never looked at what he wrote. We allowed him to use the office to write his private correspondence. He held the pen in a peculiar way. He wrote slowly. I do not recognise his writing in those letters to Chetwynd. He has not written to me. He has never signed documents in my presence. The writing in these documents does not remind me of his, nor does the writing in the book of the Galapagos Report. I could not swear to his writing. I never saw him write back-handed. I saw him about October 3rd. I believe he went to Norway after that. I believed he returned in November. I do not recollect his conversation in November, but I believe he said he had gone from Liverpool. I have not the cheques the prisoner last paid to him.

Re-examined.–His business at our office was connected with mines and other business. I remember the September cheque for £282 being cashed across the counter. I went to the bank with him.

SAMUEL ARCHER JONES.–I keep the Buckingham Hotel. The prisoner came there in September, 1893–he stayed till September, 1895. The end of 1894 and the beginning of 1895 he was shabbily dressed. He left to go to Victoria Street. His clothes were better the last month or two; I never saw him with any jewellery nor wearing white spats. No jewellery, elephants' tusks, ostrich feathers, or anything of the kind were ever brought there.

Cross-examined.–I do not know if he had a watch. We had about 40 guests at the hotel. I noticed the prisoner's dress, because I lent him a sovereign or two. I got it back. He was rather shabby up to April or May 1895. After that he seemed to be in better circumstances. He dressed better, but nothing out of the way. He had a good coat with fur on it. I saw him wear that. I do not recollect seeing a pearl pin.

MAJOR HANS RADOLPH SOFAS LINDHOLM.–I have arrived to-day from Copenhagen, whice I left two days ago. I live at Bred Garland. I am Gentleman of the Chamber of the King of Denmark. I knew Beck several years at Lima in 1880. I left Denmark for Valparaiso about May 1880. (*This evidence was objected to as not being relevant.*) I first knew Beck in June or July, 1880, and from then to 1883 or 1884. He was a good friend and an honourable man.

COLONEL HARRIS.–Beck is no friend or acquaintance of mine. I have been brought here on subpœna. I knew him in Peru from 1875 up to 1882. I have seen him with the very best class of people.

Cross-examined.–I do not think he could write two lines in English. He may have learned since. I knew he was a Norwegian. I do not think he could understand what English he did write. He spoke English very well, and Spanish remarkably well. I last saw him about five months ago in Bread Street. I had seen him twice previously; I had no business with him. I met him causally in the streets.

Re-examined.–From 1875 to 1882 I used to see him in the carriers and in the streets of Lima sometimes, and used to say "Good-day"–as one has to be careful with whom they converse in a country like that. I do not think he can write a line in English now.

FREDERICO PEZET.–I am Consul-General of Peru, in Liverpool. I knew Beck in Peru in 1880 or 1881, or before that. I have known him ever since. I have always heard every one speak very highly of him.

Cross-examined.–I knew him in London in 1894. I did not know his residence. I have seen him in the street on several occasions.

JOHN BRAILSFORD.–I live at 97, Golden Lane, Chester. I met Beck in Lima in March, 1881, afterwards in Callao up to July, 1882, and since in London; the English thought a good deal of him.

GUILTY.—*Mr. Gill applied that other indictments against the prisoner upon the file of the Court should now be tried, or that a verdict of Not Guilty should be taken upon them; as there was no authority for leaving indictments untried upon the files of the Court against the will of the person who was prepared to answer them. Mr. Avory asked the Court to sentence the prisoner upon the indictment on which he had been convicted, and to let the others be adjourned to next session, in order that the Attorney-General might be applied to to enter a nolle prosequi upon them. The Common Serjeant stated that he should not depart from a well-established practice, and that the other indictments should stand over till next session, in order that the Public Prosecutor might consider what steps should be taken.*

Four Years of the Fifth Count (charging the obtaining from Mrs. Townsend); Three Years on the Tenth Count (charging the obtaining from Madame Meissonier); these sentences to run consecutively. On each of the other Counts Three Years' Penal Servitude; to run concurrently with the previous sentence of Three Years.

−REPORT OF THE TRIAL OF MR. ADOLF BECK AT THE CENTRAL CRIMINAL COURT, CONTAINED IN THE "TIMES" NEWSPAPER OF 4TH, 5TH, AND 6TH MARCH, 1896.

(Before the COMMON SERJEANT, 3 March 1896.)

ADOLF BECK, 49, described as a Mine Owner, was indicted for obtaining rings and jewellery from various ladies by false pretences.

Mr. C. MATHEWS, Mr. HORACE AVORY, and Mr. GUY STEPHENSON prosecuted for the Treasury.

Mr. C. F. GILL and Mr. PERCIVAL CLARKE defended.

In opening the case Mr. Avory said the only question raised in the case was one of identity. A man who was alleged to be the Prisoner had systematically addressed ladies in the street, generally at the West End, calling them "Lady–" mentioning some name. He would then state that he had made a mistake, but, continuing in conversation, succeeded before he left in obtaining the address of the lady he was speaking to, and a permission that he might visit her the next day. In some cases a telegram was received from the man and this was followed by a letter from him purporting to be written from the Carlton Club, or the Grand Hotel. The man, when he arrived, introduced himself as a nobleman. He spoke of his establishment at St. John's Wood, and, stating that his housekeeper was leaving, invited the lady to take the position. He then enumerated the jewellery and dresses she would require, gave a cheque on a branch of a bank (which could not, as it turned out, be found) for a considerable amount towards the expense, and asked to be allowed to take away valuable rings so that he might be certain of the right size when purchasing the rings he had promised. In one instance, jewellery to the value of £150 was taken away. One of the ladies recognized the Prisoner as he was leaving his rooms in Victoria Street, West-minister, and gave him into custody. The Prisoner was in the habit of frequenting the smoking room of the Grand Hotel. Mr. Avory suggested that it might not be necessary to mention the name of the witnesses.

Mr. GILL said: He did not desire to have the names, as they did not affect his case in any way.

The COMMON SERJEANT said it was quite a new suggestion that a person coming forward as a witness should refrain from giving his or her name, and he must confess that he should require the authority of the High Court to induce him to alter the practice of the Court in this matter.

Mr. AVORY said he would not press that point, as the difficulties, perhaps, were not the same as when the witnesses were before the Magistrate.

The COMMON SERJEANT said he could quite understand that at the preliminary inquiry it might not be desirable to disclose the names, but this was the final inquiry.

The witnesses were then called and gave their names and addresses in the usual way.

Mr. GILL cross-examined the witnesses on the question of identity.

The hearing of the case was adjourned.

(4th March 1896.)

The trial of Adolf Beck, 49, mine owner, upon an Indictment charging him with obtaining rings and jewellery from various ladies by false pretences, was resumed.

Mr. C. MATHEWS, Mr. HORACE AVORY, and Mr. GUY STEPHENSON prosecuted for the Treasury.

Mr. C. F. GILL and Mr. PERCIVAL CLARKE defended.

Mr. Marcus Browne, proprietor of the Covent Garden Hotel, said the prisoner stayed at the hotel for about six years previous to 1894.

Mr. AVORY: Did he pay his hotel bill?

Ask my solicitors.

The witness adhered to this form of reply, and the Common Sergeant directed him to reply to the question. Mr. Browne then said the prisoner owed him an hotel bill amounting to £300 when he left, besides money borrowed.

Mr. AVORY: How much did he borrow?

That has nothing to do with the case.

The COMMON SERGEANT: Perhaps you are not aware that I have power to commit you for contempt of court, and I shall most certainly exercise my power if you are not careful. You are trifling with the court; do not let me have to caution you again.

Witness then said that the hotel bill and money borrowed amounted to £1,300 or £1,400.

In consequence of the witness's further replies.

The COMMON SERGEANT: Again interposing, said: Two of the commissioners and myself saw you deliberately wink at the prisoner when you came into the witness box, and I warn you again to be careful.

In cross-examination the witness said he brought an action against the prisoner for £1,300 or £1,400.

Mr. GILL addressed the jury for the defence, contending that the case was one of mistaken identity, and that the prisoner's conduct had been that of an absolutely innocent man.

Evidence was called for the defence with the

object of showing that at the times spoken to by the witnesses for the prosecution, the accused was wearing a dress different to that described by them; also that in October last he was in Norway. Two witnesses, one who had known the prisoner in Peru in 1880, and the other who knew him in 1875, spoke of him as an honourable man.

Mr. AVORY said the coincidences in this case were remarkable. The prisoner was identified distinctly by witnesses, who all spoke to his foreign accent, one of them having described him as a Norwegian.

The case was adjourned.

(5th March 1896.)

The trial of Adolf Beck, 49, mine owner, upon an indictment charging him with obtaining rings and jewellery from various ladies by false pretences, was resumed.

Mr. C. MATHEWS, Mr. HORACE AVORY, and Mr. GUY STEPHENSON prosecuted on behalf of the Treasury.

Mr. C. F. GILL and Mr. PERCIVAL CLARKE defended.

On the application of Mr. Gill, the prisoner was allowed to address the jury so that they might hear his voice. The prisoner said that he was absolutely innocent of these charges.

After a few minutes' deliberation, the jury found the prisoner GUILTY.

Mr. GILL then applied to have the files of the court cleared in regard to other indictments against the prisoner.

Mr. AVORY opposed the application, and asked the Common Sergeant to sentence the prisoner on the indictment on which he had been convicted and adjourn the other indictments until next Sessions, in order that he himself might apply to the Attorney-General to enter a *nolle prosequi* with regard to them. This would get rid of the difficulty.

Mr. GILL said there was no precedent for an indictment remaining on the files of the court against the will of the accused.

The COMMON SERJEANT was not inclined to depart from the well established practice of this and every other criminal court in which he had practised. Therefore he should postpone the other indictments until next Sessions, and should sentence the prisoner only on the charges of which he had been convicted. The jury had convicted the prisoner, on what he himself considered overwhelming evidence as to identity—evidence found not in one direction but in every direction—of a most base and wicked crime, one which was entirely heartless. He should sentence the prisoner on the fifth count of the indictment to four years' penal servitude, and on the tenth count to three years' penal servitude, and he should direct that these sentences should be consecutive. On the other counts of the indictment he sentenced the prisoner to three years' penal servitude, but directed that these sentences should be concurrent with the other sentences, so that the total sentence he said the prisoner would undergo was one of seven years' penal servitude.

Mr. GILL applied that a point of law might be reserved but the Common Serjeant said he entertained no shadow of doubt on the subject, and that it would be improper under the circumstances to reserve a case.

The business of the Session was concluded,

1896–1901

_PETITION FROM MR. T. DUERDIN
DUTTON ON BEHALF OF MR
ADOLF BECK, PRESENTED 20TH
MAY, 1896._

To the Right Honourable SIR MATTHEW
WHITE RIDLEY, Her Majesty's Principal Secretary
of State for the Home Department.

The Humble Petition of ADOLF BECK, a prisoner
now undergoing sentence.

SHEWETH.

(1) THAT your Petitioner was on the 3rd, 4th,
and 5th days of March, 1896 tried before Sir Forrest
Fulton, Q.C. (the Common Sergeant) and a Jury and

found guilty upon an indictment for obtaining by false pretences jewellery and other articles of value from Ottilie Meissonier and other women and sentenced to terms of imprisonment amounting to seven years' penal servitude.

(2) THAT there were also on the file of the Court several indictments for felony in each of which your Petitioner was further indicted for having on the 7th day of May, 1877, been convicted of felony and sentenced to five years' penal servitude.

(3) THAT your Petitioner desired to have this issue tried but the Counsel for the prosecution objected and the learned Judge ruled that it was not material to the issue before the Jury on the Misdemeanour indictment and the evidence thereon was entirely excluded.

(4) THAT the offences for which your Petitioner was convicted were all precisely identical in character viz. that of obtaining the goods mentioned in the Indictment by falsely representing himself to be an English nobleman and by means of false cheques.

(5) THAT the cheques put in evidence by the witnesses for the prosecution were most of them written on Bill of Exchange forms and were evidently all written by one person.

(6) THAT the case for the prosecution rested entirely upon the evidence of identity given by the women and the evidence of Mr. Gurrin the expert in hand-writing who gave evidence that in his opinion the handwriting on the cheques was the disguised handwriting of your Petitioner.

(7) THAT the ten charges preferred against your Petitioner were alleged to have been committed on ten different dates between the 3rd day of December 1894 and the 27th day of November 1895.

(8) THAT your Petitioner denies that he is guilty of any of the offences alleged to have been committed by him and affirms that the witnesses have been mistaken as to his identity.

(9) THAT in the inquiry before the Magistrate at the Westminster Police Court a retired police officer was called on the 23rd day of January 1896 to prove that your Petitioner was a man who had been convicted in the name of John Smith at the Central Criminal Court on the 7th day of May 1877 and sentenced to five years' penal servitude for a series of similar offences.

(10) THAT your Petitioner thereupon at once caused inquiries to be made with regard to the said conviction and it was then ascertained that the convict John Smith was in prison from the 28th day of April 1877 until his release from prison on the 14th April 1881 and that he was afterwards for 3 or 4 months under the care of the Discharged Prisoners' Aid Society.

(11) THAT the deposition taken against John Smith and the exhibits were also examined and it was then discovered that the prisoner in that case had adopted exactly the same course as the man who committed the offences alleged against your Petitioner, that he had represented himself to be Lord Winton-de-Willoughby and that he had given the

woman who gave evidence then cheques in the same way as described by the witnesses in the case against your Petitioner.

(12) THAT the documents attached to the depositions taken against John Smith are undoubtedly in the same handwriting as the documents produced by the witnesses against your Petitioner, the cheques being written on Bill of Exchange forms in the same way and so much alike that they might be photographs of each other.

(13) THAT Mr. Gurrin, the expert in handwriting who gave evidence at the Westminster Police Court on the 23rd day of January, 1896, states in his Report which was attached to the depositions that he examined the documents in the case of John Smith and they were undoubtedly written by the same person who wrote the documents alleged to have been written by your Petitioner.

(14) THAT all these points prove conclusively that the man who committed the offences in 1877 committed the offences alleged against your Petitioner in 1894 and 1895.

(15) THAT your Petitioner was in South America from the year 1873 until the year 1884 which embraces the whole period during which John Smith was engaged in committing the offences of which he was convicted and the time he was in prison in England.

(16) THAT your Petitioner accordingly procured the attendance on his trial of several gentlemen to prove that fact viz.: Colonel Josiah Harris, F.R.G.S.,

F.R.C.I., of 8, Union Court, Old Broad Street in the City of London who knew your Petitioner in Lima from about 1875 to 1881; John Brailsford a retired official of the Pacific Steam Navigation Company now residing at 97, Garden Lane, Cheyney Road, Chester who knew your Petitioner in the early part of the year 1881 until June 1882; Major Hans Adolf Reinhart Sophus Lindholm, a gentleman of the Chamber of His Majesty the King of Denmark residing at 49 Bredgade Copenhagen who knew your Petitioner in Peru from the year 1880 to 1884, and Frederico Alfonzo Pezet, Consul General of Peru in Liverpool residing at 14 Princes Avenue Liverpool who knew your Petitioner in Peru in 1880 and 1881.

(17) THAT all the witnesses fix their dates by the events of the war between Chili and Peru which broke out in the year 1879 and was virtually brought to a close by the Battle of Miraflores on the 15th day of January 1881 and the surrender at Lima on 17th day of January, 1881. Major Lindholm particularly remembers that your Petitioner visited him while he was imprisoned in the Prefecture at Lima six months before the surrender of Lima he having been taken prisoner by the Peruvians on arriving in the country.

(18) THAT there can be no doubt as to the correctness of the evidence of all these gentlemen and your Petitioner could not therefore be the man John Smith who was convicted in 1877 and as it is perfectly clear that all these offences have been committed by one and the same man your Petitioner

cannot be guilty of the offences for which he is now undergoing sentence.

(19) THAT your Petitioner made every effort to have these facts brought out on his trial but the prosecution successfully resisted all such endeavours and the matters stated above were not gone into.

(20) THAT the Prosecution could have included in the Indictment upon which your Petitioner was tried the previous conviction, but this was not done and upon the Indictments charging the previous conviction upon which your Petitioner claimed to be tried and upon the trial of which he would have had the opportunity of demonstrating his innocence not only of the previous conviction but also of the offences alleged against your Petitioner in 1894 and 1895, a *nolle prosequi* has been entered and in the result your Petitioner has been deprived of the means of proving that the witnesses for the prosecution were mistaken as to his identity.

YOUR PETITIONER there humbly prays:

THAT you will forthwith review the case and cause inquiries to be made into the matters herein contained with a view to preventing a grave miscarriage of justice and advise Her Most Gracious Majesty the Queen to grant your Petitioner a free pardon.

T. DUERDIN DUTTON,
40, Church Street, London, S.W.,
Solicitor for the said Adolf Beck.

–HOME OFFICE MINUTES ON THE PRECEDING PETITION

This is an attempt to get the Secretary of State to overrule the decision of a court on a point of law and then to go on to declare that the verdict is wrong.

Beck was convicted of a series of frauds on women carried out on a uniform plan. He used to introduce himself to a woman by the name of Lord Wilton and ask her to act as his housekeeper in a house at St. John's Wood. He would then give her a worthless cheque for the purpose of buying dresses, and would obtain rings on the pretext of wanting them to tell the size of her finger; sometimes he stole other ornaments or borrowed small sums of money.

He was identified with one John Smith who was convicted of similar frauds in 1877, and this former conviction was charged in the indictments.

The argument of the petition is that the handwriting of the swindler in this case is the same as that of John Smith, and all the details of the frauds are precisely similar. Therefore all the present set of frauds were committed by John Smith. But the prisoner cannot be John Smith, because he was in Peru from 1873 to 1884, while Smith was convicted in 1877. Therefore the prisoner is innocent.

Prisoner's counsel tried to raise the question of the prisoner's identity with Smith in the course of his trial, on the specific charges of fraud, but the Common Serjeant ruled that it was irrevelant. And even if the prisoner is not Smith, the evidence of his guilt in the present case is quite overwhelming. He was identified by ten women whom he had defrauded quite positively. There was also the evidence of Mr. Gurrin as to the handwriting of the forged cheques and its identity with the prisoner's writing.

A.I.E.

1.6.96.

H.B.S.

Mr. Gill tried very hard to raise and press the point now put forward in the memorial that the writing of the cheques was the writing of the man convicted in 1877, and if he had succeeded he had witnesses to prove that Beck could not be the man as he was out of the country. Mr. Avory objected and the Common Serjeant supported him. It was a clever ruse for how could his witnesses' evidence have been disproved, it would have been very difficult indeed, I should think. (See pp. 485 & 489. Sess. Paper.)

The Common Serjeant in passing sentence (Times Report, March 6, 1896) said "The jury had convicted the prisoner on what he himself considered overwhelming evidence as to identity. Evidence found not in one direction, but in every direction of a most base and wicked crime, one which was entirely heartless."

Nil

C.M.

16 June 1896.

Seen by Mr. Digby.

−PETITION OF MR. ADOLF BECK, 9TH JUNE, 1896.

NAME, ADOLF BECK.

Register No. D.W. 523.
9th June, 1896.
Chelmsford Prison.

To the Right Honourable Her Majesty's Principal Secretary of State for the Home Department.

The Petition of the above-named Prisoner Humbly Sheweth–

My Lord,—Overwhelmed with indignation and grief, with a sense of the most horrible and inhuman injustice which has overtaken me, I pray your Lordship to favour my Patition with your most careful and just consideration, inasmuch as there is not one single word of truth in the whole of the accusations brought against me.

I solemnly declare, that I never saw any of thise women, nor the Chequs which has been produced by them, until I saw them at Westminster Police Court. The hand-writing on thise Cheques, but not the signatur, which I saw at the Police Court, is somewhat similar to my own, but I have seen a good many other peoples writing, more so than this.

Besids those proofs given at the trial for my defens, ther were several more which were not produced. The reason of thes would be to long to explain in this Petition.

Unfortunately I cannot write English correctly, without assistance, or a dictionary I therefor humbly ask your Lordship to kindly send someone to whom I can verbally explain the whole truth so far as I know it, of my case, so that it may be properly brought before your notice.

I also earnestly ask that your Lordship will have my body examined by the Doctor here, because certain scars were svooren to, as belonging to me, and also one under the ear which I do not posses, but for which the Judge in sentencing added 3 years.

Another monstrous accusation was swooren to be a Policeman, that he, "beyond the shadow of a douth,"

I was the man he took prisoner (giving the name of Smith) in May 1877, and who was sentences to five years penal servitude, for exactly the same sort of offence. Why! was defence refused by the Judge against this accusation?

From what I have heard, ther can be no doubt that this Person who ever he is, is the same who hase committed the crime for which I am accused by this Woman.

Your Lordship will find, that in examining that man's triel of '77, ther will be found the same story as told by thise Woman against me, the same Cheques, the same handwriting and signatur.

Besides the testimonials given at my trial of four gentlemen who knew me at that period at Lima (Peru) I can bring your Lordship any amounts of proofs, that I never left that country from 74 till 84. Why! am I here with a symbol, namly, letter D, which I am told signify former conviction?–when I have never been convicted befor in my life.

If this my most dreadful situation is due to misidentity, I certainly cannot help thinking that there is a Plot carefully laid by enemies taking advantage of same.

After it was to late to alter, I know that the solicitor who has been acting for me (Mr. Dutton) was sent to me by thos enemies.

I asked to see my Council (Mr. Gill) before the trial commenced; this Mr. Dutton refused.

Immediatily after my sentence (5th of March) I asked him to draw up a Petition, for me to sign, he having all the particulars, and also of that man Smith's trial of 77. I have waited patiently, but this is also refused.

I pray your Lordship to kindly give me permission to write to the Swedesh and Norwegian Ambassador in London, as I have Property and Interest in my native Land Norway and in London, for which I need his immediate assistance, under the circumstances under which I am placed.

In whatsoever situation, misfortune, or foults I may have had, I have never been guilty of obtaing anything by false pretences, nor have I ever stolen the value of a half-penny from Man or Woman in my lifetime.

Surely I have suffered sufficient (since the 16th of Debr, ulmo) in regards expenditure, torture of imprisonment, and ruination, for othere Peoples Treachery, Villany, and crime.

For the sake of humanity and rightiousness, I sincerely pray and trust that your Lordship will give Justice to your Petitioner and humble servant.

ADOLF BECK
8th June 1896.

[NOTE.–On this Petition there was a Statement by the Governor of the Prison that the Prisoner had in the name of John Smith been previously convicted on May 7th, 1877, at the Central Criminal Court of stealing rings, and had been sentenced to 5 years' penal servitude.]

"To the Under Secretary of State, Home Office,

Whitehall, S.W.

"*Re* ADOLF BECK.

"Churton Street, London, S.W.,

May 25th, 1898.

"SIR,

"Referring to my letter of the 16th instant respecting the above, I have been informed that it is believed the man John Smith, *alias* Ivan Weissenfells was of the Jewish persuasion, and would therefore have been circumcised in accordance with the custom of his race. I do not know whether this appears on the records of John Smith, but it can of course be easily proved that Beck has not been circumcised.

"It can also be easily proved that Beck is a Norwegian subject and a copy of his Certificate of Baptism obtained and evidence produced to show that he is the man referred to therein, whereas I am informed that Smith or Weissenfells, was not a Norwegian subject.

"I have the honour to be, Sir,

"Your obedient Servant"

(Signed)   T. DUERDIN DUTTON."

–LETTER DATED 12TH MAY, 1898, FROM THE PRISON COMMISSIONERS TO THE GOVERNOR OF PORTLAND PRISON, AND THE MINUTES MADE THEREON.

Prison Commission,
Home Office, Whitehall,
12th May, 1898.

To the Governor, Portland Prison.
D. W. 523 ADOLF BECK.

Please forward the Penal Records for the above named convict.

(Signed)   E. G. CLAYTON,
                                                    Secretary.

Minutes made on the above letter.

(i.)

Noted. Penal Record herewith.

(Signed)   B. PARTRIDGE,
                                        Governor of Portland Prison,
                                                    13.5.98.

(ii.)

Penal Record returned. Be so good as to have this prisoner's description revised carefully. The marks, &c., shown do not agree with those on the old Penal Record. Send up a full description after marks, &c., have been retaken.

(Signed)   E. G. CLAYTON,
                                Secretary to the Prison Commissioners,
                                                    14.5.98.

(iii.)

Marks retaken and inserted in description. It appears from a statement by the Medical Officer on an application to change religion, dated 13.1.79, in the case of D. 523 John Smith, that this prisoner had been circumcised. I requested the Medical Officer to examine D.W. 523 A. Beck, and enclose his report, from which it will be seen that Beck has not been circumcised.

Penal Record returned.

(Signed)   B. PARTRIDGE,
                                 Governor of Portland Prison
                                                 19.5.98

*Copy of the Report of the Medical Officer mentioned in the
above Minuts:–*

*The Governor, Portland Prison, To the Medical Officer,
Portland Prison.*
D.W. 523.   ADOLF BECK.

Will you be good enough to inform me if the above-
named prisoner is circumcised.

(Signed)   B. PARTRIDGE,
                                                 Governor.

The Medical Officer, Portland Prison, to The
Governor, Portland Prison.
        No. He has certainly not been circumcised.

(Signed)   O. M. MADWELL, M.O.
                                                 18.5.98.

–NOTE OF THE DISTINCTIVE MARKS OF JOHN SMITH AND ADOLF BECK.

	JOHN SMITH.	ADOLF BECK.
Complexion	Dark	Fresh.
Hair	Brown	Grey.
Eyes	Brown	Blue.
Height	5 ft. 6 ins.	5 ft. 63/8 ins.
Build	Proportionate	Proportionate.
Shape of Face	Oval	Oval.
Marks–		
Right Side	Scar bottom lip.	
	Scar upper part of nose.	
	Scar jaw.	
	Two vaccination marks.	
	Scar outside arm	Long scar front of upper arm.

	Mole arm pit.	
		Scar head.
		Small mole neck and nape of neck.
		Boil scar above shoulder blade.
		Slight scar front shin.
Left Side	Mole neck	
	Mole shoulder	
	Three vaccination marks	
		Scar cheek.
		Slight scar front shin.
		First joint fourth finger slightly contracted.
	Circumcised	Not circumcised.

–HOME OFFICE MINUTES: MAY AND JUNE, 1898

(i.)

I believe Mr. Dutton is so far right that Beck and Smith are different persons which is shown by the marks on them which I have compared and which differ widely and which curiously have never been referred to before: but this does not prove that Beck was not guilty of the many offences of the same kind of which he was convicted, he having been satisfactorily identified by numerous women whom he had defrauded; though it does prove that the police witness was mistaken and shows how invaluable in such a case would have been the measurement system.

C.M. 23 May 1898.

(ii.)

It is a very curious case but the evidence of Beck's identity by the numerous women he had defrauded was positive. I have seen Inspector Froest who was examined at the trial, and he says that the evidence of the women was overwhelming.

The fact of Smith's circumcision was ascertained when he applied for leave to change his religion to the Jewish.

Though the present conviction is not affected by the representations made by Mr. Dutton, I think the papers should go to the Common Serjeant for his opinion and observation.

C. M. 27 June 1898.

I agree. K.E.D. June 29 '98.

–PETITION OF MR. ADOLF BECK, DATED 5TH JULY, 1898.

Name–ADOLF BECK.

5th July, 1898.   Register No., D.W. 523,
                                   Portland Prison.

To the Right Honourable Her Majesty's Principal Secretary of State for the Home Department.

The Petition of the above named Prisoner Humbly Sheweth–

In reference to my previous petitions–I beg to

correct an error, as to the statement made of the year of my birth, in saying 1844 instead of it being 1841.–The mistake is due to a misunderstanding of a statment made to me when one a vicit home afther my arrival from Feru.

From the beginning of this most terrible, and unparralleld injustice–which has befallen me, I have asked for my certificat of baptism to be sent for.–But, as I am entirely in the hands of a conspiracy.–it was only product to me a few days ago, by their Agent Mr. Dutton. Such are,–and have been my bitter experience throughout my case.

I have only now been told,–that I have been chandestinely slandered–by certain personal enemies–this is also very hard on me,–being deprived as I am, of any advocacy for demand of Justice against such–and likewise of my case.

Apart from the many statements made of my innocence, in my previous petitions–there can be no doubt–as the inspection of my marks of identity now have been accomplished–and by the Medical Officer here,–that it will surely give to your Rt. Hon. Sir, more infallible proofs of my entire innocence,–As it will fully prove–that I have no scar on my neck–as alleged by some of these women,–and for whom I was sentenced–and never seen before I saw them at Westminster Police Court–It will also fully prove–that I am not a Jew,–as I am told the man is for whom I bear the letter D.–and whose trial of 1877, was read to me at the Old Bailey, by Mr. Duttons clerk.

Convinced, as I trust your Rt. Hon. Sir, will be by now, that I am not the man convicted in 1877–but that I abode at Lima–which were confirmed by honourable gentlemen who knew me there, and identified me at the Old Bailey.

With all such indisputable facts,–I most respectfully pray your Rt. Hon. Sir, to take the accusations made against me at Westminster police court,–and those of the man convicted in 1877, under the name of Smith,–for whom I am accused to be,–lay them side by side,–then certainly it will be seen, and give another most palpable proof, of that all these accusations alleged to me,–is nothing else but a most infamous fabrication of falsehood from beginning to end.

In reflecting upon the manner in which the whole proceedings of this case, have been conducted against me,–I cannot help feeling convinced, that it is a conspiracy, organized, and formed, with these women out of Smith case–by somebody under the influence and bribe of an enemy–whose purpose have been, to inflict upon me my most terrible sufferings–and to ruin and plunder–of my business matters and belongings.

By Him who knows the truth of all things–and from whom no secrets are hid.–I pray Your Rt. Hon. Sir to have compassion–and bestow righteousness upon me, to exonerate and release me–.as I am innocent of every crime imputed to me.

Your humble servant
ADOLF BECK.
June 30th 1898.

[NOTE.–On this Petition there was a Statement by the Governor of the Prison that the Prisoner had in the name of John Smith been previously convicted on May 7th, 1877, at the Central Criminal Court of stealing rings, and had been sentenced to 5 years' penal servitude.]

–CORRESPONDENCE BETWEEN THE HOME OFFICE AND THE COMMON SERJEANT IN JULY, 1898.

Letter from Home Office to Common Serjeant.

Whitehall,   8th July, 1898.

"SIR,

"I AM directed by the Secretary of State to transmit herewith a petition received at this Office in May 1896, on behalf of Adolf Beck, a prisoner under sentence of seven years' penal servitude, together with the Central Criminal Court Sessions. Papers containing a report of his trial and also a report of the trial of John Smith in May, 1877, to which reference is made in the petition; also five petitions of different dates from Beck himself, a petition from John Smith dated 25th June, 1879, and a letter received from him in May, 1881, two further communications from Mr. Duerdin Dutton of the 16th and 25th May last, and a note of the distinctive: marks found on John

Smith in April, 1881, and Adolf Beck at the present time.

"Sir Matthew Ridley would be much obliged for your opinion on the case, generally and especially on the representations made in Beck's behalf.

"I am,

"Sir,

"Your obedient Servant,

"(Signed)   CHARLES S. MURDOCH.

   "The Common Serjeant

            of the City of London."

Letter from Common Serjeant to Home Office.

27, Queen's Gardens,
Lancaster Gate, W.

Re ADOLF BECK.

SIR,

13th July, 1898.

THIS man was tried before me on March 3rd, 4th, and 5th, 1896, and after a patient trial was convicted of having defrauded a number of women of loose character. The evidence of his identity was most overwhelming, all the witnesses to identity picking him out from a number of others, without the slightest hesitation. The convict had the great advantage of being defended by Mr. C. F. Gill, but although a most skilful cross-examiner he was quite unable to shake any of the witnesses. There is an error in the report in the Sessions Paper, at page 475–the witness Brakefield did not, it is true, succeed in finding the little scar by the right side of the neck under the ear spoken to by her, and described as something like a mole, but this was due to the fact that in the dock he was wearing a collar and scarf, whereas at the time that she saw the scar Beck was partially undressed. At my instance a more thorough examination was made by the warder, who at once found a small scar or mole mentioned in the description. Again at my request Brakefield looked at this mark and said "Oh yes, of course that's it"; to my mind this in itself was a most damning piece of evidence, as also was that of Frank Cooper, corroborating Fanny Nutt, and proving that Beck had been for some years the constant frequenter of the smoking room at the Grand Hotel, Charing Cross. It is, of course, untrue, as stated by the prisoner in one of his petitions, that the jury were informed before verdict that the prisoner had been previously con-victed on the 7th of May, 1877, and sentenced to penal servitude for a similar offence. In passing sen-tence I distinctly stated that I should sentence the prisoner only for the offences for which he had been convicted before me. I did not investigate the ques-tion as to whether he was John Smith, although I have very little doubt that he and Beck were one and the same person. I do not understand if the paper sent to me purporting to be a record of the marks on the person of Smith and Beck respectively is official or not. I observe that Mr. Dutton in one of his commu-nications says he is informed that Smith was a Jew and was circumcised. It is of course obvious that if at the time of his conviction Smith was circumcised, and Beck is not so, they cannot be one and the same person. With respect to the South American alibi, I should be inclined to regard it with great suspicion, particularly having regard to the source from which it comes, and I should myself require the most stringent and searching examination before I acted upon it in any way. I regarded this crime as of an exceptionally cowardly, selfish, and cruel nature, and fully deserving the no doubt very severe sentence I passed upon him. The reason I did not investigate the circumstances attending the identity of Smith and Beck are fully explained and set out in the report of the case in the Sessions Papers.

I am, Sir,

Your Obedient Servant,

(Signed) FORREST FULTON.

To the Right Honourable

    Sir M. W. Ridley, M.P.,

       Secretary of State.

–HOME OFFICE MINUTE. JULY, 1898.

July, 1898.

The Common Serjeant has not the slightest doubt that Beck is the man who robbed the women in 1895; whether he is also the man who was convicted of a similar offence in 1877 is open to doubt, but this is really immaterial as Beck is being punished only for the offence proved in 1896.

Nil: But let convict be given a fresh prison number so that his identity with John Smith should not be affirmed. H. B. S., 15.7.1898.

C. M., July 18, 1898.

K. E. D., July 20, 1898.

[NOTE.–In August, 1898, a fresh number "W. 78" was assigned to Mr. Beck in place of his former number "D. W. 523."]

–LETTER FROM HOME OFFICE TO MR. DUERDIN DUTTON. 27TH JULY, 1898.

Whitehall,

27th July, 1898.

SIR,

In reply to your application on behalf of Adolf Beck who is undergoing a sentence of seven years' penal servitude, I am directed to inform you that after very careful consideration of all the circumstances of the case, the Secretary of State does not feel justified in recommending any interference with the sentence passed in this case.

I am,

Sir,

Your obedient Servant,

(Signed)   CHARLES S. MURDOCH.

T. Duerdin Dutton, Esq.,

      Churton Street,

         S.W.

–PETITION OF MR. ADOLF BECK, 29TH AUGUST, 1899.

Name.–ADOLF BECK.

H.M. Prison, Portland.

Register No. W. 78.

29th Aug., 1899.

To the Right Honourable Her Majesty's Principal Secretary of State for the Home Department.

The Petition of the above-named Prisoner Humbly Sheweth–

To give a full account of all I have been forced to witness during my captivity, vould fill several foolscaps, and for my disability in writing–especially upon such trickesh tangle–defamation and per-jure–must be left for a legal adviser–when I am at liberty to see him. But, in my nine previous petitions, I thought I had clearly demonstrated, enough to show, that this whole affair is a conspiracy, a got-up case, dobtless to my belief, with hired women, and by the aid of the police official, who swore me convicted by the name of Smith, in London 1877 for identical offence, whilst I was living in Peru, and by looking into these two cases–no person can fail to see therein–full evidence of my above statement–which is admited to be so, by the alteration of my marks of sentence, from D.W. to W. last August, and why the W. still remains, I fail to understand and beg for an expla-nation. Since then, inspection of my neck have been made by the Medical Officer here, and fully proved, that I have no scar, as alleged to me by these women.

In addition, (if there is an atom of truth in Mr. Dutton) amongst proofs of my innocence not produced at my trial–, Mr. Dutton now declares to me 29th April ult.: that he have handed to your Rt. Hon. Sir, a cheque given by the same man to a woman in London, in October 1895 during my stay in Norway. Surely all this speaks for itself.

To describe and view–more fully my painful experience in this case, I beg to lay a few questions before your Rt. Hon. Sir.

Is it just and legal? for persecute with the most infamous false accusations–and for its purpose–use false witnesses produced from an other mans case–and lay them upon any man–a complot, or a plotter–may choose to assault, and most probable, his principal motive for so doing is to fulfil his bargain with that man's enemy.

Is it just and legal? for a police official, or any person to defame, and swear falsely against any man in a sacred court of justice.

It is just and legal? for persecutors and plotters party, after seizure of their prey, to forward their Solicitor, to impose and intrud upon prisoner as his Solicitor, for to play his part in concert with them, and to hinder prisoner from procuring honest succour.

It is just and legal? for any Solicitor to withhold evident proofs of prisoners' innocence from his trial, and reject his informations, and 'let false statements pass unopposed, but this Solicitor to act entirely to his own purpose, by feign and farce, and all sorts of trickery, so as to mislead the public from the truth of the case, and to this effect, he also instructs his Counsel, to whom, his falsely accused victim, is denied to informe on his case. And from what I have seen, this mode of acting is also continued in his petitions, and in his article in the "Morning" masqurading under the name of Sims, which article commences its heading by an insult.

Is it just and legal?—by such means and method, to criminate any man as the lowest criminal of criminals, to his total disgrace and ruination, and thereby sell him as a slave, for also to plunder, ruin, and bereave him of his business matters, money and property.

These are a few outlines of this monster complot, in which Mr. Dutton have acted as chief abettor to them who lead these false witnesses against me, and enemies behind the scene, promoters of this outrageous plot.

Being thus prosecuted, Mr. Dutton first helps himselfs out of my property with about £375 cash.

Then for my interest of several thousand pounds in a valuable patent, his grate endeavour was to force me to give it up for £100. The following year his proposal was £1,500 which I refused. Since then I hear no more of it, as he render no account of anything. Likewise his designs is to treat with my copper property in Norway for a song.

Concerning my other business matters, as I hope have not fallen into his hands, which documents are in the City, I can only know of them—when it pleases your Rt. Hon. Sir to allow it—as my communication for such, to honourable men, has not been allowed me, even so to my legation in London.

By all these circumstances, and grounds of facts, I again beg your Rt. Hon. Sir, to grant an exonerated release to your most humble Petitioner.

ADOLF BECK.
24th of August, 1899.

[NOTE.—This Petition contained a statement that the prisoner had never been previously convicted.]

–PETITION OF MR. ADOLF BECK, 4TH NOVEMBER, 1889.

Name.—ADOLF BECK.

Register No. W. 78
H.M. Prison, Portland,
4th November, 1899.

To the Right Honourable Her Majesty's Principal Secretary of State for the Home Department.

The Petition of the above-named Prisoner Humbly Sheweth—

I am now nearly four years a prisoner—innocent of every word uttered—and all in connection therewith—in every charge made before me—by everyone of these women—and the policeman. All of them, including Mr. Dutton, intirely unknown to me before my arrest.

Of this my terrible position—I have laid before

your Rt. Hon. Sir, as much proofs–as it is possible in my present position–being entirely in the hands of my adversaris–and deprived of any outside help for my vindication–as explained in my petition of 24th August ult.–And for to give another proof of the truth–of my statements therein–I implore Your Rt. Hon. Sir to reconsider my petition of 28th September ult. with regard to the Cheque.

I only ask for what is due, and just–and given to every human being throughout the civilised World.

As I was released from the letter D, so do I trust to be from W–it is only Justice.

For this I ever pray–and hope your Rt. Hon. Sir, will give–to your most abused and victimised petitiner.

ADOLF BECK.

November 2nd, 1899.

P.S.

My Petitions are dated as follows.

No. 1.	20th July	96
,, 2.	8th April	97
,, 3.	3rd June97	
,, 4.	15th July	,,
,, 5.	26th August	,,
,, 6.	27th October	,,
,, 7.	30th June	98
,, 8.	6th October	,,,
,, 9.	10th November	,,
,, 10.	1st December	,,
,, 11.	24th August	99
,, 12.	28th December	,,

[NOTE.–These two Petitions contained a statement that the prisoner had never been previously convicted.]

–DESCRIPTION OF ADOLF BECK AS RELEASED ON LICENSE,

8th July, 1901.

Date and place of birth	1844, Norway.
Height (without shoes)	5. ft. 6 in.
Complexion	Fresh.
Hair	Grey.
Eyes	Blue.
Trade or occupation	Nil.
Married or Single	Single.

Descriptive marks or peculiarities:–

Left.–First joint fourth finger slightly contracted, scar on cheek, forehead, and front shin.

Right.–Long scar front upper arm, boil scar above shoulder blade, scar front shin, cut scar side of head.

Mole right side and nape of neck, two small moles on chest.

1904

*-EXTRACTS FROM THE BRIEF
DELIVERED BY THE DIRECTOR
OF PUBLIC PROSECUTIONS TO
COUNSEL TO PROSECUTE IN THE
CASE OF THE KING AGAINST
ADOLF BECK, JUNE, 1904.*

Central Criminal Court Sessions, commencing the
20th June, 1904.

THE KING V. ADOLF BECK.

Brief for the Prosecution.

The prisoner stands committed for trial at these
Sessions upon charges of obtaining money and goods

by false pretences and of larceny. Five separate cases were investigated at the police court, and each of the prisoner's victims has fully identified him as the offender. The defence is an alibi, and the prisoner was asked in the usual way if he wished to give evidence, but although he called upon Heaven to witness and the Press to take note that he was an innocent man, he did not venture to go into the witness box.

The facts of the case are fully set out in the depositions, and there is no necessity to recapitulate them here. This will be the third time upon which the prisoner has stood in the dock at the Central Criminal Court charged with offences of a like description. Counsel will find in the Sessions Papers of 1876–7, page 51, and 1895–6, page 462, a complete account of his past misdeeds and his *modus operandi*.

–AFFIDAVIT OF ALBERT YEO, IN OPPOSITION TO APPLICATION FOR POSTPONEMENT OF MR. BECK'S TRIAL.

REX ADOLF BECK.

I, ALBERT YEO, Detective Sergeant, "F" Division Metropolitan Police, make oath and say as follows:–

1. I am one of the officers in charge of this case and it is part of my duty to see that the witnesses attend the court.

2. The principal witnesses for the prosecution are: Pauline Scott, Rose Reece, Lily King, Caroline Singer

and Grace Campbell, who, as the prosecution allege, have all been defrauded by Beck.

3. The above mentioned witnesses have already attended from four to six hearings of this case at Marylebone Police Court, and have attended two days at the Central Criminal Court in the discharge of a public duty and at great inconvenience to themselves.

4. Pauline Scott informs me and I verily believe that it was owing to her having to attend the police court to give evidence against Beck that she had to leave her situation as a domestic servant at Hampstead and that if she is compelled to attend at the Central Criminal Court next July or at some other future date she will lose her present situation as domestic servant at Scarborough.

5. Rose Reece informs me and I verily believe that she is housekeeper to a family who will be leaving this country for the Continent on the 9th July next and that she will not be back in this country until the end of September next.

6. Lily King informs me and I verily believe that she will be leaving England for Belgium on or about the 30th of June instant and that her return to this country is very uncertain.

7. Caroline Singer informs me, and I verily believe that she will be leaving this country in about eight days' time to join her husband in Belgium and that she will not return to England.

8. The remaining available witness who has been defrauded by Beck is Grace Campbell, who is now dangerously ill and cannot leave her room.

9. The witnesses above-mentioned, with the exception of Grace Campbell, say that they are willing, in the interests of justice, to stop in London another week if necessary, in addition to the time they have already lost over this prosecution, but that they should not be compelled to attend the court at some distant date, merely to suit the convenience of Beck.

10. The said Adolf Beck has not produced any evidence or shown that he will be in a position to employ a solicitor in his defence if the trial is postponed to some future date.

Sworn at 45, Ludgate Hill, in the
City of London, this 22nd day
of June, 1904

Before me   } (Signed) ALBERT YEO.
P. HEDDERWICK,
A Commissioner for Oaths.

–REPORT OF THE TRIAL OF ADOLF BECK AT THE CENTRAL CRIMINAL COURT ON THE 27TH JUNE, 1904, CONTAINED IN THE CENTRAL CRIMINAL COURT SESSIONS PAPERS. VOL. 140, 1ST PAGE 764.

Old Court–Monday, June 27th, 1904.
Bèfore Mr. JUSTICE GRANTHAM.

ADOLF BECK (63). Unlawfully and fraudulently obtaining by false pretences from Rose Reece a gold ring, from Pauline Scott a watch, a ring and £1, from Grace Campbell a ring, from Lily King a ring and 4s., and from Caroline Singer £2, with intent to defraud.

MR. MATHEWS, MR. BODKIN, MR. BIRON, and MR. STEPHENSON, Prosecuted; and MR. LEYCESTER, Defended.

ROSE REECE. In August, 1903, I was living in Marylebone Road–I was then out of an engagement–one afternoon in that month I was near Oxford Circus–the prisoner spoke to me–I swear he is the man–he said he had seen me on one or two occasions before, and was desirous of making my acquaintance–that he had only five minutes to spare, would I kindly give him my address!–silly like, I gave to him–in the hurry I did not think there was any harm in it–about a week afterwards I received a letter in writing like this one (*Produced*)–it had "Hotel Victoria" stamped on it–I have destroyed it–it said, "Will call upon you at 4,30 in the afternoon to-mor-row"–nobody came, but about six weeks afterwards the prisoner called and said, "You remember receiv-ing a letter from the Hotel Victoria"–I said I did, and asked him in, because he said he was interested in me, and would like to know something about me–I told him I was a housekeeper out of an engagement, but was looking for one–he said he had a large house in St. John's Wood, and wanted a housekeeper–I thought it was a good opportunity–he did not describe the house, except to say that he had a cook and a house-maid there– he said I should require some dresses, as I was then rather badly off for them–I was to get a tai-

lor-made dress–I cannot remember each one, but he
made a list in pencil–the writing was similar to this
list, but the amount was different–I was to get the
dresses at Madame Haywards', in Bond Street–he said
he thought that would be a nice place to go to, as he
had got many dresses there and was known there–he
saw I had a little ring on my finger, and he asked
whether I would like another–I said I should–he
asked if the one I had on fitted me well–I said it
did–he said he would take it for the measurement–he
did so–it had a design of a shamrock in the centre and
three diamonds and a ruby on either side–it was
worth about £4–I had had it for some time–he asked
me what sort I would like, and I said a diamond and
turquoise–he said it should be so, and that it would
come from Streeter's in Bond Street–he wrote me out
a cheque for the dresses for £74–it was similar to this
document–he would not let me see it, but sealed it up
in an envelope, and addressed it to the Union of
London Bank, Pall Mall–he would not let me see the
signature–I tried to see it, and asked him if he would
tell me what it was–I tried to look over his shoulder,
but he put his arm up, and said I was to take it just as
it was to the bank–I saw that it was written on a half
sheet of notepaper which I gave him–I said, "Had not
you better write it on a cheque form?"–he said,
"Immediately they see my signature they will give
you the money"–he took the ring off my finger; I did
not give it to him–I cannot say if he did so before or
after he wrote the cheque–I should not have let him
take my ring away if I had not believed his story–I

begged him to be careful not to lose it, because it was a present from my mother–he made a pretence to give it back to me, but did not do so–I let him take it away as he promised to return it the following morning–next day I went to find the Union Bank in Pall Mall–I asked several policemen, but they said there was not one there; the nearest one was in Cockspur Street–I went there and presented the cheque–before that I had steamed the envelope open and looked inside and then closed it– that is how I know it was like this cheque–I could not make the signature out–the cheque was not honoured at the bank–I never saw my ring again, and I did not see the prisoner until I picked him out of a number of other men, I believe, at Paddington Green Police Station, about April 23rd–I gave the police a description of the man who had swindled me.

Cross-examined. When I picked him out I believed he was already in custody on Miss Scott's charge–I did not particularly notice the other men when I picked him out–I believe all of them were younger than he is–I cannot remember if any of them had grey moustachious–I caught sight of the prisoner immediately–I had never seen the man who robbed me before August, and upon that occasion I was only with him about five minutes, talking in the street; it was about 5 p.m.–I did not see him again until October–I saw him then for just an hour–I did not see him after that until April 23rd–I do not remember if anything was said when I picked him out–his nose is most peculiar, and is one I could pick out of a thousand–his whole face is different from any other man I ever remember seeing–when he came to me he had on a jacket suit of black and fawn small check–it was not a dark suit, but rather light, and had white spots–he had no overcoat–I think when I picked him out he had on a brown suit, not a blue one, as he has now, but I am not certain–I looked at his face, not his dress–I think he had eyeglasses on then–the man who robbed me was not wearing eyeglasses when he came to see me–I cannot quite remember if he put them on to write–I kept all the documents until the Friday before he was arrested, when I tore them up–I am positive about the writing–it slopes backwards, which is rather peculiar–I have seen German writing sloping like that–I do not think it is often seen in English writing–I remember the signature perfectly–nobody can read it, and that is what makes me remember it.

Re-examined.–I have never seen a signature like it before–I have not the slightest doubt that the prisoner is the man who robbed me.

PAULINE SCOTT. On March 22nd I was living at 27, Cambridge Terrace–on that day I was in Oxford Street–the prisoner came up and spoke to me–he asked for my address, and if I would like to meet him again–I gave him my address–he said he was staying at the Hyde Park Hotel–next day I had this letter from him (*Produced*); it is written on Hyde Park Hotel notepaper: (*Read*) "My dear Miss Scott,–I shall have pleasure in calling to-morrow between 1 and 2.–Yours——"–the signature I cannot make out–he called next day–he said he would like to make me a little present, as he was interested in me–he wrote out this list of dresses, which I was to get (*Produced*)–he said he was a lord, I do not remember the name, I think he said Willoughby– he said he could not stay long as he had to go to the House of Lords–he wrote out this cheque (*produced*) to pay for the dresses; it is written on an ordinary sheet of notepaper–he asked me to get the paper, as his valet had forgotten to put his cheque-book into his pocket–he put it into this envelope, but did not seal it up–he asked me if I would like some jewellery–I said I should–he told me he would send me some, and asked me if I would like a ring, and if I had one to take as a measurement–I gave him one and he said it would do very nicely–it was not a very expensive one–the prisoner asked had I not got a better one, which would fit me better–I said I had not–he asked me it I would like a watch–I said I had one, but it was out of repair–he asked me to let him see it–I showed it to him–he said, "It is a nice little watch; I will take it and have it repaired for you"–the watch and the ring were not very valu-able–I have had the watch ever since I was a child–I then said I was going out to have some lunch–he said he would come with me, but he had got no money on him–I had my purse which he took, and took a sovereign out, and said, "This will pay for the lunch"–we went, and got to Edgware Road–he said, "I think you had better get into a cab and drive to the bank, or it will be closed–he did not have any lunch–I got into a cab and drove to the bank–I got there and found the cheque was not good–that was between 1 and 2 p.m.–I did not remember the banks did not close till 4 p.m.–the prisoner said it was quite a mistake that he had got no money, that he had got up late, and his valet had forgotten to put any in his pocket–I did not get my lunch, but the prisoner got my watch and ring–I then went to Scotland Yard and gave a description of the man who had swindled me–I afterwards received information from the police, and went to a restaurant at 35, Oxford Street–I did not recognise the prisoner there–as a matter of fact that night I felt so nervous I could not have spoken to him even if he had been there–I saw somebody who I thought was like him; he was wearing glasses then, but not when I met him–I was in rather an awkward position behind a partition, and could not see him–the morning he was arrested he had glasses on, and I recognised him quite well–on April 15th I was with Detective Ward, waiting at the corner of a street in Tottenham Court Road, I do not know the name–I saw the prisoner; I went over to him and asked him what he had done with my jewellery–I said, "You are the man who took my jewellery and my sovereign"–he said, "No, I am not; I do not know you; I have never seen you in my life before"–I said, "You are the man took my jewellery"–he said, "Who put you up to this? You come with me to my solicitors"–I said, "I have got somebody waiting for you here"–he tried to make off round the corner, but of course Mr. Ward came up and took him to the station.

Cross-examined.–The prisoner kept on denying

that he had ever seen me before–that was the first thing he said when I stopped him–I expected to see the prisoner there–I think it was at the corner of South Street–I did not see the prisoner come out of a house–he was going to pass me without taking any notice of me–I never saw him before March 22nd–on that day he was only with me a few minutes in the street–it was between 5 and 6 p.m.–the next time I saw him was at my lodgings about 1.10 p.m.–I only saw him for five or ten minutes on that day–he was not wearing spectacles or glasses at that time–I think he wrote the cheque and list without using glasses, but I am not quite sure about that; I did not look at him while he was writing–he was dressed in a dark overcoat, a bowler hat and spats, and I think he had a light overcoat–I did not see him without an overcoat, so I do not know what he had on underneath– I do not know if he had a velvet collar–on April 15th he was dressed as he is now; he had no overcoat then–I think he was wearing eyeglasses then, but I am not sure– I have seen him since, in custody, without glasses–at the police-station he was told to take them off–he wore them until he was told to take them off–I went to the restaurant in Oxford Street on March 31st with Ward–I went in and sat down–I did not notice if the prisoner was standing talking to the proprietor when I went in–I went there to see if I could see the man who had robbed me–I do not think he was there when I went in–I looked round to see if he was there–I saw a man talking to the proprietor– I believe now it was the proprietor–I did not quite

re...
the ...
at the ...
oner—I st...
hours—I do...
time—the man...
not know how ...
have not the least ...
hour—Ward was not ...
outside—I did not notice ...
had glasses on then.

LILY KING.—I live at .... Mansions,
Piccadilly—in March I lived ......, Gloucester
Mansions, Cambridge Circus—On March 28th, about
8 p.m., I was in Regent Street—the prisoner ask me
for my address—I gave him a card—next day I got this
letter: (*Read*) "Hyde Park Hotel, Monday evening.
My dear Mrs. King—Please expect me to-morrow,
Tuesday, between one and two o'clock," with this signature which is illegible—this is the envelope—next day
the prisoner called between one and two—I saw him
in my sitting-room he offered to take me to his
house—he said he had two servants, but I should feel
lonely because he had no time—he said I could not go
to his house as I was, and that I should have to have
some dresses—he said he was a lord, and had a house
in the country, with a fruit garden and a wine cellar—he wrote out a list of dresses amounting to
£230—he wrote me out a cheque for £250—at first it
was £225, then he said, "Do you owe something?"—I
said, "a couple of quid," and he said, "I will make it

[partially obscured rotated text] ... they wo... ... rings—he put it into an envelope ... measurement—... he asked for one... "£250," but I did not see the che...

—I saw him writing
que—I was wearing some
he took a plain gold one as a
he said he would buy me some, and
would arrive at four o'clock that day—he left the
house—I was to go quick to the bank—he told me to
give my servant half-a-sovereign, which I did—he said
he had not got half-a-sovereign himself, as his servant
had not put any money into his pocket— he borrowed
the half-sovereign from me to give to my servant—he
said, "I have not got any change about me; have you
got any?"—I said, "Yes, but I have only got 4s."—he
said, "give it to me"—he took it and the ring—I went
right away to the Union Bank, Knightsbridge—I did
not get the cheque cashed—I think the prisoner was
wearing glasses, but I am not sure—I afterwards saw
him at the Court with a number of other men and
picked him out.

Cross-examined.—He was then in custody—I
noticed the other people he was standing with; I
think about nine or ten were there—I think they were
all younger than the prisoner—I do not think there
was anybody else there with a grey moustache—I told
the police the man who robbed me had a grey moustache—I do not know if I mentioned that he wore
glasses—I did not remember anything about his wearing glasses until I was asked about it at the
Police-court—I never saw him before March 28th—I
only saw him for a few minutes on that day—and for
about half-an-hour on the next day—those are the
only times I saw him—he was dressed in dark

clothes–he had a dark black overcoat on–I did not notice the collar–he said he was a lord, but he did not say what his name was–he spoke in English–I cannot speak English very well–I did not talk any German to the man who robbed me.

DR. BOYD.–I practice at 118, Seymour Place. I saw Grace Campbell at 23, Quebeck Street, Wardour Street, this morning. She is unable to leave her bed, and has been unable to do so for the last ten days, in consequence of the state of her health.

WARD (Police Inspector).–I was present at the Police-court when Grace Campbell gave her evidence in the presence of the prisoner. He had an opportunity of cross-examining her. She signed her deposition as well as the Magistrate (*Deposition read*): "I live at 123, Quebeck Street, Wardour Street. I am single and of independent means. In February I was in Albemarle Street. It was between February 24th and 28th, between 4 and 5 p.m. I had been to an office. As I was going away the prisoner spoke to me. I was quite alone. I had seen him before I went into the office in the Arcade between Bond Street and Albemarle Street. As I came out he spoke to me in a most gentlemanly manner. He said, 'I have seen you somewhere before. ' I said 'Probably you have. ' He said he had seen me in Scotland. I am Scotch. I asked him who he was. He said he was a friend of the Sassoons in Park Lane. He said he would like to take me out to lunch, and asked my name and address. I gave it to him. I told him I did not want my people to know I had done so. He said he did not want his to know either, as he was a great lord. He did not tell me what his nationality was. I had a letter next morning which I at once tore up; it bore the address of the Albemarle Hotel, where the prisoner said he had stayed some months. It was in exactly the same printing as exhibit 7. He called at the address I gave him next day as I was finishing luncheon. The friend I was staying with came in for a moment while he was there. Prisoner only stayed a few minutes. He said he had a house at Abbey Road, St. John's Wood, with servants. He said he had a lady friend staying there, and asked me to take her place. I declined. I was wearing two diamond rings. He looked at them, and said they were not good enough for me, and he would get ever so many grand rings from Streeter's in Bond Street for me. He asked me to let him see my half-hoop diamond ring for a pattern and to show the size. I let him see it and went and spoke to my friend in the next room. When I returned I did not want to part with it, and he gave it back to me. Eventually I let him take a plain gold ring, which I told him had belonged to my mother. He said, 'You don't trust me? ' I said, 'Well, I don't for a gentleman does not usually ask a lady for a diamond ring to act as a pattern. ' He took away the plain gold ring. It was worth about £1. He said I should have a great many dresses as a present, and I was to get them from Hayward's in Bond Street. He wrote out a list of them on a piece of paper, and read it to me. He took one list away and left one with me, which I destroyed. The handwriting it was written in was exactly similar to that on document marked 3, but my list was much more sumptuous, and the dresses were to cost £250. He wrote out a cheque for that amount, and said I was to take it as a present. It was on plain paper on the Union Bank, St. James's. He left it in a envelope sealed up. He told me not to touch it but to go to the Union Bank, St. James's Street next morning. I destroyed that cheque directly he had gone. It was in exactly the same writing as that marked 2. He told me to stay in till 6.30 p.m., because he would go to Streeter's and get my rings, and would sent them to me by commissionaire. I never received any ring nor my own back. I never took the cheque to the bank. I never heard from him again. Last Saturday I picked the prisoner out from a great many other men I have not a doubt he is the man."

Cross-examined.–At first I believed in him, but when he asked for my ring I suspected him–I never thought the cheque was genuine–I never expected to see my ring back. When I saw him first I only talked to him for a few minutes. The interview at my friend's only lasted half an hour–he had a dark grey overcoat and patent leather boots on a foulard tie with a cheap pearl pin–I can identify the prisoner by his general appearance, back and front from top to bottom–the men he was placed among were all younger than the prisoner–the man who called on me wore eyeglasses and a pair of gold pince-nez.

CAROLINE SINGER (Interpreted.)–In March I was living at 4, Keppel Street I recollect meeting a man in Oxford Street who asked if he might go home with me–he asked for a card; as I had not got one I gave him my address–some days afterwards. I received this letter (*produced*.)–the man called next day which was Sunday–he said, "I am very rich, and have got plenty of money"–he wanted me to go to his house–I said, "I am married"–he said, "It makes no difference; I want you as a friend"–we spoke in English–he made out this list–he wrote this cheque for £140 to pay my debts–he said, "I am going to buy you a chain and watch and a pair of diamond earrings, and a marquise ring"–he said, "Give me those earrings as a pattern"–he pointed to the ones I have on now–I said, "No, I cannot give you these, they belonged to my mother who is dead"–he borrowed £2 from me–I told him it was given me by my husband–he did not say what he wanted the £2 for–I picked him out at the police court–the prisoner is the man.

Cross-examined.–I only saw the man twice–I spoke two or three words with him in the street–I do not speak English very well–I did not speak any German to him–the second time I was with him for about thirty minutes–he said, "I do not speak anything else but English"–he had a single eyeglass hanging down, but he did not put it on–he had a brown suit on a black overcoat with a velvet collar–I picked him out on the same day that the others did.

WALTER ELLIOTT MURPHY. I am a cashier at the Union of London and Smith's Bank, Charing Cross branch–we have no branch in Pall Mall–cheques like these have been presented at our bank for payment for nearly a year–they were always presented by women–about twenty or twenty-five have been pre-

sented—in none of them can we decipher the name of
the drawer—if the signature is a name, no such person
has an account with us—all the cheques were dishonoured—none of them were on proper cheque
forms—some of them were drawn on Union Bank, St.
James's Street—we have no branch there or at
Knightsbridge—we have one in Sloane Square—I do
not know the prisoner—none of the cheques have a
stamp on.

WILFRED STAGG. I am a clerk in the inquiry office
at the Hyde Park Hotel, Albert Gate—these letters are
written on Hyde Park Hotel notepaper, which is left
in the public room for the use of visitors—anyone
coming into the room can write a letter on that
paper—I have not seen the prisoner at the hotel.

Cross-examined. There is an attendant whose duty
it is to notice people coming in—I look after the visitors' mail and so on—if the prisoner came in I think I
should notice him.

STEPHEN DE MARIA. I keep a restaurant at 35,
Oxford Street, and have known the prisoner for two
and a half years as Adolf Michael Beck—he constantly
came in as a customer and had his meals there—after I
had known him about six months he asked me if I
would allow his letters to my place—I said, "Yes,"—they
came addressed to Adolf Beck, except on one occasion,, when it was Michael Adolph Beck—he said he
was engaged in the city as a commission agent—he had
breakfast at my restaurant, and sometimes lunch, but
not lately, and every evening he had dinner—for the
first few months he paid every day, then he told me

he was rather short, and I said, "I have no objection, you can go on and pay me whenever you can"–at present he owes me between £40 and £50–I remember some time before April the police coming and speaking to me at my Holborn shop–I saw the prisoner the same day–I did not then mention that the police had been to me–on April 4th when he came to my place about 8 a.m. he said that when he went to his hotel the night previous somebody told him that the police were after him, and that the proprietor would not allow him to sleep there any longer–he was then sleeping at the Percy Hotel, Percy Street–I said, "I do not think there is anything against you, because the police came to my place, and Inspector Ward said there was nothing against you"–I think the prisoner said, "I am not going to be looked upon as a dishonest man; I had better leave; I shall look out for a room and I shall leave"–he said he wanted to be free and easy, and did not want to be locked up–he said he moved to 7 or 9, South Crescent.

Cross-examined. He asked me who the police officer was, and I showed him Ward's card–he asked me to go to the station with him, which I did on Easter Monday–there were several constables there, but Ward was out, so I made an appointment to meet him at 2.30 that afternoon–I saw him about the prisoner's case–the prisoner was not there then, but he afterwards asked me, "Have you been up there?"–I said, "Yes,"–he said, "What did he say?"–I said, "He had nothing against you, but only wanted to know where you lived"–when the prisoner moved to South

Crescent I believe he left his address with me—I knew his address all the time he used my house—I was quite willing to give him credit—I am not complaining that he swindled me; he always paid me before—I remember Miss Scott coming to my restaurant one evening—the prisoner was there having some tea, I believe—he was there for about one and a half hours while she was there—I noticed that she was looking at the table where the prisoner and I were sitting—she was looking at him; there was nothing to prevent her seeing him—I believe that was on March 21st, but I am not sure.

Re-examined.—On the first occasion I went with the prisoner to the police-station at his suggestion—he waited outside because I asked him to—I went to see if there was anything against him.

WILLIAM GREEN.—I am manager of the Central Hotel, Percy Street—I know the prisoner as Adolf Beck—he stayed at the hotel from October 16th to October 30th, 1902, from November 14th to 17th, 1902, from December 28th, 1902, to January 20th, 1903, and from February 14th, 1903, to April 4th, 1904, when he finally left—I understood him to be an agent—when he left he owed 30s.—he was requested to leave, although I did not give him notice myself—people had been inquring for him.

Cross-examined.—It was the police who had been there, and I did not like it. It was after he had stayed at the hotel from February 1903, to April 1904 that he owed 39s.—I am not making any complaint that he had swindled me.

JAMES WALTER PALMER.–On April 24th I lived at 9, South Crescent–I remember the prisoner taking a room at 10s. a week–he said he had come from the north, that he had been living at an hotel, and wanted a cheaper place–he said he was a financial agent, and that his name was Adolf Beck–he stayed until he was arrested–his effects were taken charge of by the police.

WARD (*Re-examined*).–On March 24th I received information of Miss Scott's complaint–I called upon her and took her statement–she gave me a description of the man she said had robbed her–I made inquiries and communicated with De Maria–I ascertained that the prisoner was living at 9, South Crescent–on April 15th I told Miss Scott to stand at the corner of Store Street, and if she saw anybody she knew, or the man who had stolen her jewellery, to speak to him–about 9.30 the prisoner came out and looked round at Miss Scott–they spoke for a few minutes–I went across the road, and she gave him into custody as the man who had stolen her jewellery–he said, "It is a mistake"–I said I was a police-officer, and he would have to go with me to the police-station–I conveyed him to the station, and when he was charged he said it was a trumped-up affair–he gave De Maria's address as his own–I told him it was false, and that he was not living there–he said he was–I said he was not, and I directed the inspector who was taking the charge not to put it on the charge sheet–The prisoner said he was an agent and a Norwegian–after he was charged he asked to send a telegram, and in my presence he wrote these four telegrams and this envelope—I found 2s. 4d. in money on him and a number of articles, among them being two pairs of eyeglasses—I made a list of the articles—I afterwards went to 9, South Crescent, and took possession of his effects—I made a list of the things; it contains pince-nez; keys, a box containing visiting-cards, pawn tickets, hair-dye, two pocket-books, an overcoat, a washing-book, and some memoranda in this envelope—on the 23rd April I placed the prisoner with twelve other men at the police-court; some were about his own age, some older, and some younger—I told him he was about to be put up for identification, and that he could stand where he liked, he chose his position, standing with his back to the window—he was going to take off his coat—I told him not to do so, as other people were wearing coats—he had on a greatcoat with a velvet collar—he was wearing glasses, and I told him to take them off, as other people were not wearing glasses—the witnesses came in separately, and each picked him out—in each case he said he did not know them—he was wearing a hard felt hat.

Cross-examined.—The witnesses are wrong if they say the prisoner was wearing glasses when they identified him—I do not know that the man who committed the robbery did not wear glasses—I seized everything that I could find at the prisoners's lodgings—I found a light grey suit: there were eight or nine suits there—this is the overcoat he was wearing—produced—there is no velvet collar on it; I am wrong about that—I am not wrong about his wearing glasses, because I told him to take them off–a woman was brought in to identify him for a different offence altogether; she did not do so–I did not find any pawntickets relating to any of these articles, and I have not succeeded in tracing any of them to him–De Maria told me he took his food at his place–I did not know that De Maria knew where he lived.

THOMAS HENRY GURRIN.–I am an expert in handwriting at Bath House, Holborn Viaduct–I have practised for about twenty years and have given evidence for the Treasury and others, hundreds of times–I have seen the exhibits in this case–I have compared the list of dresses, cheques, and letters addressed to the witnesses, with the telegrams and envelopes proved to be in the prisoner's writing–to the best of my belief the writing on those exhibits is the studiously disguised writing of the same person who wrote the five proved exhibits–some of the disguised writing is written backwards, some of it straight, and most of it is distorted in such a way as to suggest that it is intentionally disguised–I see in it a number of peculiarities which I see in the proved writing–I should say the handwriting belongs to the Scandinavian group, Norwegian or Danish–I have occasion to study manuscripts of foreigners, and I have noticed the t's and f's of that writing–I have also compared the disguised writing with a pocket-book found at the prisoner's lodgings–almost all the writing in that book is the same as that which appears on the telegrams, and it is the same writing as the other exhibits, only they are disguised.

Cross-examined. The pocket-book supplied me with a great deal more material—the style of writing is foreign—I do not think there is any instance in the disguised writing where it is absolutely natural, except by inadvertence—I think it was all intended to be disguised—all the capital P's in the telegrams have the same peculiarity—the umbrella part goes through the main stroke—in the disguised writing there are eight P's, and in most of them one sees the same peculiarity—there are many differences in the writing, but, to the best of my belief, they are not material.

Re-examined. The dissimilarities are not what I should expect to find in the writing of two different people.

The prisoner's statement before the Magistrate. "Before God, my Maker, I am absolutely innocent of every charge brought against me. I have not spoken to or seen any of these women before they were set against me by the detectives. I can bring many witnesses to prove I have acted honestly in my business in the City from 10 a.m. to 6 p.m. I ask the Press to help me to get all evidence in my support from my solicitor."

The prisoner in his defence on oath said he did not know any of the women; that he had never seen them: that on March 22nd he was in the City doing business with a Mr. Gajardo from 11 to 3, and stayed in the City till 6 p.m.; that he was in Mr. Williams', his solicitor's office in the afternoon; that he had dinner at De Maria's between 6 and 7; that on March 23rd he was in the City at lunch-time; that on March

28th he was with Gajardo all day on business; that he remembered Miss Scott. being in De Maria's restaurant on March 30th; that on 29th March he had lunch at a baker's shop in Old Broad Street; that the letters to the witnesses were not written by him; that he could not write without glasses, and then not more than two sentences in English without using a dictionary; that he carried two pairs of pince-nez, one for distance and one for reading; that he had been mistaken for a man named Smith, his double; that in March and April he had no brown suit, or a coat with a velvet collar; that he was receiving £3 or £4 a week from Mr. Williams; and that he received an option on some copper property of his own in Norway.

Evidence for the Defence

MATHEW EDWARD WILLIAMS.–I am a Solicitor of Board Street Place, Finsbury Circus–I have known the prisoner for fifteen years–I have taken up his defence during the last week only–I know his writing–I have received a number of letters from him–in the course of my profession I deal with handwriting–I have seen the letters written by the thief–I say most decidedly they are not written by the prisoner–I do not trace the slightest resemblance–the characteristics of the two writings are entirely distinct in my opinion–during March and April I made the prisoner an allowance–I was engaged in the sale of property for him–I have the contract here–I made him an allowance because of that property, and because I had known him a long time and had a respect for him–I should think I have given him £200, on an average of £2 a week–there were no regular payments–I was prepared to lend him anything within reason–I have never seen him without eye-glasses, except to wipe his eyes–I imagine that he cannot write without them–I have never seen him write, except to copy letters written by my clerk.

Cross-examined.–I made him an allowance because I believed he wanted money, and because I believed that it would be repaid–I do not do that for anybody who asks it–the prisoner was introduced to me by some clients–his property is a series of mines, described in this agreement of sale–I have not seen him, but I have corresponded with our agent in Christiania concerning them, and he has seen the title–I have a list of my payments–I have no receipts except the cheques–towards the end of last year I received about £200 from the prisoner, which was part of £500 paid on his property–I did not know that I should be called as a witness until ten minutes ago–I was rather anxious to be called in the prisoner's interest–I had a good deal of experience in hand writing in my early days–I was never employed in comparing handwriting–Mr. Gurrin's business is to compare handwriting hypercritically; mine is to get a general contour of the whole thing.

By the Court.–I knew of this case some weeks ago, but not professionally–it was after Mr. Freke Palmer was not able to continue it that I took it up.

Guilty.

—He then Pleaded that he had previously also been found Guilty to a conviction of obtaining goods by false pretences at this Court on February 24th, 1896.

ADOLF BECK

THE INQUIRY

"I wanted to go into the witness-box and tell the whole story of John Smith, but they would not let me. The Clerk of the court said I had been formerly convicted, I began to speak and said that in my defence I was innocent then as I am innocent now, and it stopped the Judge, who postponed sentence to next Session. I was sent to Brixton Prison.

On the 9th or 10th July John Smith was brought there, and Mr. Williams told me. The governor got to hear it, and took him out of the hall where I was, but I saw him at chapel two or three times. There is no resemblance between us. I saw the scar on his chin and the wart on his eye."

DESCRIPTION of WILLIAM THOMAS, alias JOHN SMITH, arrested 7th July, 1904.

Complexion	Fresh.
Hair	Grey.
Eyes	Hazel.
Height	5 ft. 5_ ins.
Build	Stoutish.
Face	Oval.
Age	Says 65.
Place of Birth	Lincolnshire.
Trade	Journalist.

Distinctive marks, &c.:–

Right side.–Faint scar on bottom lip, one on upper part of nose, one on upper part of jaw, two vaccination marks on left arm; scar outside arm, mole on armpit left side, eight large moles and numerous small on neck and shoulder, three vaccination marks on right arm, circumcised, scar on right cheek and between eyebrows. Circumcised.

MEMORANDUM by Mr. T. H. GURRIN, dated the 18th July, 1904.

Re ADOLF BECK.

Inspector Kane,

Hearing that you are in charge of the case against William Thomas, alias John Smith, I have to report that having seen and examined the letter and envelope dated July 6th, 1904, produced in this case, I identify it beyond any doubt as being the same handwriting as the incriminating documents produced in the John Smith case 1877, and Beck's cases, 1896 and 1904.

Adolf Beck's writing and the writing in these documents are of a similar foreign type and share resemblances which led me to conclude that the 1896 and 1904 documents were in Beck's disguised writing.

I am now satisfied that this deduction was inaccurate.

I may add that in both the trials 1896 and 1904 I maintained that the incriminating documents were identical with the documents in the case of John Smith in 1877.

(Signed) THOMAS HENRY GURRIN.

July 18th, 1904.

The Inquiry

Sergt. JOHN WATTS, called and examined.

The CHAIRMAN: What are you?–I am a detective sergeant of the A division of the Metropolitan Police. In 1895, my Lord, I was detective constable stationed at Rochester Row Police Station, and had an inquiry from Daisy Grant—

You are going almost too quickly. I want to ask you a little more. How long have you been in the Service?–$18\frac{1}{2}$ years.

You began, I suppose, as a police constable?–Yes, I was just over six years a uniform constable, my Lord, and four years a detective constable, and I have since risen from a third-class sergeant to a first-class sergeant.

Have you had any bad marks against you?–Not in the whole of my career, my Lord.

And you have been how many years do you say?–$18\frac{1}{2}$ years.

You were a police constable in 1895, were you?–A detective constable

And you were at the police station at Rochester Row?–Yes.

Who would be your superior at that station?–Local Inspector Waldock.

He would be your superior?–Yes, also the inspector in charge of the police station.

As it happened, were you told that on the evening in question, the woman Meissonier was brought to the station with Mr. Beck by a constable?–Yes, Constable Edwards, a uniform constable.

And you happened to be the person in authority, the senior officer in charge of the station at the time?–Yes, my Lord, I will explain. I was making inquiries then. I had received a complaint in July from Mrs. Grant, of Wellington Chambers, York Street. That was in my district.

Before you go to that, you happened to be the senior officer in charge of the station when Mr. Beck was brought in there by Constable Edwards?–No, there was a uniform Inspector in charge of the station.

Was he actually in charge of the station at the time?–Yes.

Who was he?–I believe it was Inspector Pigott, who is now pensioned.

Edwards brought Mr. Beck along with Ottilie Meissonier to the station?–Yes.

What happened then?–The Inspector told me a few of the circumstances; that Mr. Beck was brought in on a charge of stealing jewellery from Madame Meissonier,

You were not personally present when Mr. Beck was brought in?–No, I think I came in about 10 minutes afterwards.

The inspector having seen Beck and Meissonier?–Yes. I said I had a similar inquiry. We keep a record, what we call the felony book, where all particulars of crimes are entered; and I showed the inspector, this entry in our felony book that Mrs. Grant had complained of this jewellery, so the inspector directed me to find Mrs. Grant to see if she could identify Mr. Beck. I went to Wellington Chambers, York Street, the address she had given when she had made her complaint, and I ascertained she had gone to live at 44; Circus Road, St. John's Wood. I then went to St. John's Wood, and found Mrs. Grant. She returned with me to Rochester Row Police Station the same evening, and in the meantime Mary Harvey had arrived at the police station.

That is Meissonier's servant?–Yes, Meissonier's servant. When I arrived at the police station I informed the inspector on duty that I had found Mrs. Grant and a number of men were brought in from the street.

Who was responsible for that?–I brought the men and the inspector was present.

What was the inspector's name again?–Pigott. Mr. Beck was placed with a number of men.

Had you selected the men? Where had you found them?–In the street or adjoining shops. The procedure is this. When a prisoner is brought to a police station on a charge of stealing property, we try to get men somewhat similar as near as possible, and to get them from the street or from shops, or anyone who will come in, and the person who is detained is then asked by the officer on duty if he is satisfied with the men that he is placed with. If the man says, "No I am not satisfied," then we get some more men, and the person accused is allowed to stand wherever he likes in a line of men. He is told he can place himself where he likes and he does so. Sometimes a man may be brought in, and there are several witnesses. There is only one witness allowed to go into the room at a time for the identification, and the accused person probably might be picked out by the first witness. If the accused likes he can then shift his position and stand at the other end, or in the middle, or wherever he likes. Mr. Beck was placed with a number of other men.

Do you remember how many men?–I believe it was about seven, and Mr. Beck said that he was innocent and did not mind where he stood. The first witness that came in was Grant. I was present and the constable and also Mr. Pigott. The witness Grant came in and she went to Mr. Beck and said "I believe that is the man, but I should know if he took his hat off," and all the men present then took off their hats and

Mrs. Grant said he was the man who had stolen her rings. Then Miss Harvey—

What became of Mrs. Grant when Miss Harvey came in?–I cannot quite recollect. Mrs. Grant would probably stand on one side then. She may not have left the room, but she would have no communication with the other witness Harvey.

There was no opportunity of speaking to the witness previously?–No.

You take care to provide against that?–Yes, we do not allow the witness to go back into the same room where the other witnesses are.

Do you take the precaution that they do not stand near each other when they do come into the same room?–Yes, my Lord. This woman Harvey also identified Mr. Beck, and then he was charged with stealing the rings.

That was the whole of the identification process at the time?–Yes, at the time.

I suppose you gave evidence at the trial, did you not?–Yes, my Lord.

Were you cross-examined by Mr. Gill?–Yes.

I mean you were cross-examined as to the mode in which you had conducted the identification?–Yes, and before Mr. Beck was placed in the cells on the charge of stealing this jewellery from Daisy Grant I searched him myself, and found upon him a £10 note, a £5 note.

I do not trouble you about that; it is not material. Did you conduct any identification besides this one?–No; Local Inspector Waldock did.

Then all you had to do was with the identification by Mrs. Grant and by the woman Harvey?–Yes.

That is the only identification that you were responsible for?–Yes.

Sir JOHN EDGE: As a matter of fact, neither on Mr. Beck nor in his lodgings in Victoria Street was anything found which was connected with any of the charges?–Nothing whatever. I made a most careful search.

Nothing was found that was connected with any of the charges preferred by any of the women?–No.

The CHAIRMAN: That is throughout the whole of the case none of the missing articles were traced to Mr. Beck?–No; and no cheque, or anything.

Though all efforts were made at the time to trace them?–Yes, my Lord.

(Adjourned for a short time.)

Mr. GEORGE WALDOCK, called and examined.

The CHAIRMAN: What are you?–I am an Ex-Inspector of the A Division of the Metropolitan Police. I am retired after 30 years' service.

You were 30 years in the service?–25 years out of that a detective.

I suppose detective is a higher rank than that of an ordinary constable?–Yes, my Lord, you obtain it by qualification.

You are promoted from the first to the second?–Yes, my Lord.

We are told that you had to do with certain identifications in the case of Mr. Beck.–Yes, my Lord.

Will you just tell us what the occasions were, and then how they were conducted?–In the first place, I may say I had known Mr. Beck for about three years prior to December, 1895. Rochester Row Police Station, that is the police station where he was given into custody by Miss Meissonier, was one of the stations of which I had charge, being in the A Division, and it was usual for me to visit that station perhaps once or twice a day. On the evening he was given into custody by Miss Meissonier I happened to go into the station some short time afterwards and was surprised to see Mr. Beck detained there accused of robbing this woman. Knowing me, of course he appealed to me as being innocent, but the woman swore to him, and I said, well, of course, I was very much surprised to see him there. However the woman swore to him and insisted upon charging him, and there was no alternative but for the inspector to charge him. I think Mrs. Grant and Miss Meissonier's servant had attended and identified him. It was after that that I went into the station.

They had been at the station and identified Mr. Beck before you came back?–Yes, I had nothing to do with that identification at all.

That was under Watts' own control or that of, I think, Mr. Pigott?–Inspector Pigott. Mr. Beck appeared before the magistrate the following morning and was remanded in custody. There were several remands and during the remands inquiries were made and a number of women came forward to identify him. I arranged the identification. Mr. Beck arrived at the police station in the prison van in the usual way, and the chief clerk to Mr. Dutton, the solicitor, was there to receive him to take instructions from him. These women were all in the police station, out of view of the van altogether.

You were responsible?–I was then superintending, and responsible for the identification, being the Inspector of the Division. After Mr. Burgess, that is Mr. Dutton's chief clerk, had done with Mr. Beck, he was brought out. I got, I think, 15 or 16 other men resembling Mr. Beck as much as I could; having regard to knowing him so long, I took particular precaution, because I knew him so long, and I took every precaution I possibly could.

In choosing the men?–Exactly. We arranged them, and I asked Mr. Beck if he was satisfied. He said, "Perfectly ; I am innocent. It don't matter if you put me anywhere. I am perfectly satisfied." Mr. Burgess, Mr. Dutton's clerk, I thought well to have present, so that he could see for himself what took place at the identification, and what happened. After arranging the men the women were called in one by one to identify him; here are the remarks which they made. I reported afterwards to the Commissioners, and it subsequently went to the Treasury. The women came in one by one, and when one woman had been in, that woman was sent on one side and not allowed to speak to the one who was to be called in next.

You took steps to prevent the one who had been in talking to the one who came in?–Yes, my Lord, this is what happened in the matter. I reported this on the

12th January, it appears to be dated. "I have known the prisoner Adolf Beck for the last three years. On or about 2nd January, 1893, I interviewed him at Covent Garden Hotel, referring to a man," so and so, "whom I subsequently arrested for" so and so. "Since then I have frequently seen Mr. Beck in the neighbourhood of the Strand, Charing Cross, Whitehall, Royal Aquarium and Victoria Street. I was present at Westminster Police Court yard on the 2nd January, 1896," that is the day I speak of, "when prisoner was placed with about 14 to 16 other men for identification. I told him to place himself where he liked. He replied: 'I am perfectly satisfied.' The following witnesses were then called one by one to identify him. Miss Sinclair pointed to prisoner and said: 'That is as much like the man as any of them. I believe he is the man.' Miss Vincent pointed to prisoner and said: 'I feel almost sure he is the man.' Miss Johnson pointed to prisoner and said: 'That is as much like the man as any, but I should not like to swear he is the man.' Miss Taylor at once pointed to the prisoner and said: 'That is the man, I can swear to him. I have no doubt about his being the man.' I then told prisoner" (that is Mr. Beck) "that he would be charged with stealing property from at least three of the above. He replied: 'I have never seen one of the women before to my knowledge, so help me God.' "

Did you give evidence at the trial?—No, my Lord. Then the case developed so very much and I was the local inspector of the Division and had the divisional matters to attend to. The Treasury then wrote to Dr.

Anderson, then Assistant Commissioner of the Criminal Investigation Department, asking for the service of an officer there who could devote his whole time to the matter.

We have heard that?–I did no more in the matter after that.

You were not called as a witness at the trial?–No, my Lord.

I suppose some of the women whose identification you speak to were called?–Yes, my Lord. Taylor specially was one.

She was cross examined, as we know, by Mr. Gill at the trial?–I could not say that, my Lord. I did not go to the Sessions at all. I gave no evidence at the Police Court or the trial.

I think two of them were called, but you do not know?–I do not know, my Lord.

So far as you were concerned I understand that you took every possible precaution to make the identification a fair one?–Absolutely, having regard to knowing Mr. Beck for three years and seeing him frequently about the neighbourhood.

The Witness withdrew.
Chief Inspector FRANK FROEST, called and examined.

The CHAIRMAN: Are you still in the Service?–I am Chief Inspector of the Criminal Investigation Department.

We have heard that you were responsible for two

of these identification processes?–Yes, my Lord.

Will you just tell us what took place in each of them–what you did so as to secure a fair opportunity of identifying?–It was done entirely under my supervision, and I was assisted in the identification by Sergeants Watts and Allan. Watts, knowing the neighbourhood, procured people from the outside, who volunteered to go into the courtyard. The women who attended to identify the prisoner were kept in the station, and they were allowed to go out into the courtyard of the court one at a time. There were four women attended, and four women identified him, and as they went out and identified him they were taken straight into the court before the magistrate.

So as to avoid all possibility of conversation?–Yes. In all cases of identification the greatest care is taken so that one witness could not possibly have any conversation with another one who was about to go in for identification.

So as to avoid all possibility of conversation?–Yes. In all cases of identification the greatest care is taken so that one witness could not possibly have any conversation with another one who was about to go in for identification.

Will you, in your own language, just describe that incident of seeing the scar and so on?–There was Madame Meissonier and there was a Kate Brakefield. I am not quite sure that I saw Madame Meissonier's identification, because the witnesses were out of Court. I certainly saw Brakefield's. She told the judge, and it was the first time that we knew it, that this man, she thought, under the collar of the shirt had a scar. The judge ordered that the prisoner should be taken below and examined by the warder. He went below and brought the prisoner up with his shirt and collar loose. I am not clear as to what the warder said. Whether he said he saw it or not, I am not quite sure, but the prisoner was holding his face one way, and turned to speak to the jury, and one of the jury said: "Why, I can see the scar there," and the jurymen got up and looked, and they appeared to be satisfied they saw something, and there the incident ended. I did not see the scar myself. I was sitting behind counsel on the other side of the Court.

The jury were in the jury box?–They were in the jury box, on the right side to the prisoner. The judge was sitting in *that* direction, the prisoner was *here* and the jury was *there*. I was sitting at the back of counsel on *this* side.

He turned towards the jury?–He turned towards the jury, and as the head turned in *that* direction they were satisfied that they saw some scar somewhere on *this* side.

Inspector ALFRED WARD, called and examined.

You are an inspector?–I am an inspector.

How long have you been in the Service?–17 years.

You were promoted, I suppose, from the ranks to the position you now hold?–Yes, my Lord.

You conducted, I think, three identification processes in this matter?–Yes.

Will you just tell us the circumstances?–The first identification was that of Miss Scott; that is where she identified him in the street.

Just tell us shortly about that?–I took up this inquiry, and according to our police records, I came to the conclusion that the person whose arrest was sought was Mr. Beck. I ascertained he used to frequent a restaurant in Oxford Street.

This was in 1904?–This was in 1904, and I requested the woman Scott to go to the restaurant. She went there on the 30th March. She remained some time, I should think for an hour. I remained outside with another officer. When she came out of the restaurant I asked her if she had seen anyone there who had robbed her. She said no. Some time elapsed then, I think about a fortnight or something like that, until I ascertained that Beck was living at Store Street, Tottenham Court Road. On the morning of the 15th April I accompanied Miss Scott to Tottenham Court Road and I placed her at the corner of Store Street, and I told her if she saw anyone come along the road that she recognised as the man who had taken her jewellery to speak to him. About 9.30 in the morning Beck came from Store Street, and she stopped and spoke to him. They were talking for about five minutes. I crossed over the road. She said: "This is the man who stole my jewellery and took my sovereign from me." I told Beck that I was a police officer, and that I should take him into custody on that charge. He said: "It is all a mistake." I said: "You hear what the woman has said. You will have to accompany me to the police station." And I took him to Paddington Police Station. After he was charged, he said it was all a trumped-up affair. He appeared before the magistrate and was remanded, and during the remand we received a communication from the Treasury asking to see me. This was on the 16th. I saw Mr. Sims on the 18th, and he asked me how many cases there were against Beck, and I said at present only one and, he said if there were any other cases the Director of Public Prosecutions would be prepared to take the matter up. During the remand there were other complaints. We received that of the women Reece and Singer. Singer went to the Tottenham Court Road Police Station. Reece came to Paddington Police Station, and the girl Campbell also came to Paddington Station. Their statements were taken and reduced to writing, and on the remand Mr. Beck was put up for identification in the usual way. There were some 16 or 17 persons selected from those whom we could get round the Court. Some were older and some were younger and some were as much like him as we were able to get. After these men were in the room, I may tell you that the women, of course, were in the matron's room, so that they could not see any of the persons who passed through the court into the prisoner's room, and that room was in charge of Sergeant Yeo. After the men had got into the room I went down to the cell and got Beck, and I told him that we were going to place him up for identification, and that he had a perfect right to stand where he chose. He said, "I do not care where I stand. I am perfectly innocent." I said, "Well, now, that is your matter. You stand where you like. There are a number of men here; you stand where you like." He said, "Well, I will stand here," choosing his own position. At that time most of the men that we had were wearing coats. He pulled off his coat. I told him to put it on, and I said to him, "Now, we want to be fair to you, and we want you to be fair to us. We do not want to have any difference about the identification," and he put his coat on and remained so. He said, "I do not care." I remained in the room. The witnesses were brought in one by one, and they each of them identified Beck as the man who had robbed them. Beck was further charged with these three offences and appeared before the magistrate. I do not think on that occasion any evidence was given. He was further remanded for a week or eight days or something of that, at the request of the Treasury. During that remand another case came to our knowledge, that of the girl King, and I saw her. Someone wrote to Scotland Yard about her. I saw her and took her statement, in company with Sergeant Yeo, and on the 7th she attended at Marylebone Police Court, and I again saw Beck, and he was placed with about eight other men who were prisoners, most of them, and I then told him that he was going to be placed up for identification again, and he had a perfect right to stand where he chose. He said: "I do not care where I stand. You will tell them where I am standing." I said: "Do not say that, because I am not going out. It does not matter to me. I am impartial in the matter. You stand where you like." He said: "I do not care where I stand." He chose his own position, and the woman King, who was brought forward to identify him, did identify him.

Where were the women brought from?–There was only one on that occasion. She was brought from the matron's room, I did not fetch her myself, but a gaoler did. She identified him, and of course he was further charged with that, and again remanded. Then on a subsequent occasion there was another complaint received, and Beck was put up for identification again, and this woman failed to identify him. She said that he was a man quite six inches taller than Beck, and a bigger man altogether. That deals with the identifications, my Lord.

That is all the identifications?–That is all the identifications, my Lord.

You are an officer of old standing, and have been promoted to the position you are now in for merit. Did you take every possible precaution to prevent any communication or suggestion between the witnesses and anyone?–I did.

You were there yourself?–Yes.

Are you satisfied that nothing of the kind took place?–I am perfectly satisfied. I am perfectly sure that nothing of the kind took place.

Was it possible, in your judgement?–It was not possible, because as the women came in they were kept in the room. They had no opportunity of getting out.

Mr. THOMAS HENRY GURRIN, called and Examined.

The CHAIRMAN: I understand you desire to make a statement?–That is so, my Lord.

You were the expert in handwriting who gave evidence at the first trial of Mr. Beck?–I was, my Lord.

Would you like the Secretary to read your statement, or would you prefer to read it yourself?–I think I would prefer to read it myself. The documents in the charge against Mr. Beck were sent to me from the

Treasury in December, 1895, and January, 1896. They consisted of the incriminating documents and of specimens of Mr. Beck's handwriting. I submitted them all to a careful analysis, and made various tracings for the purpose of comparison. I do not think it would serve any useful purpose were I to endeavour to show all the grounds on which I based the opinion I then gave, but I may briefly say that the two groups of writing differed in general appearance, Mr. Beck's being more uniform and usually sloping forward, while the other was apparently distorted and written backward, vertically, and forward. I need not say that a difference in general appearance cannot be relied on as showing different authorship, because if a writing be disguised, the aim of the writer has been to produce an effect as distinct as possible from that produced by his ordinary writing, and in such cases if the penmanship does not absolutely baffle detection, the authorship may be identified by the tracing of peculiarities and habits existing in proved handwriting and inadvertently left in the disguised writing. The distorted forms of many of the letters and the variety of angle and style in the incriminating documents, as well as their fraudulent nature, led me to assume that they were disguised. The handwriting in these incriminating documents contained a number of peculiar features. It appeared to be a foreign hand, the capitals particularly being suggestive of types commonly met with in German, Norwegian, and Swedish writings. In Mr. Beck's writing I found features which seemed to me to be of a kindred type. In both groups of writing I found a similar variety in the size of the capitals, varying from large to very small. In both I found resemblances in various letters, capital and small, as well as in some of the figures–3, 4, and 5–which seemed to indicate the habit of the same writer. The consideration of these resemblances led me to the belief that the two groups of writing were by the same hand, only that in the one case they were disguised. This was the result of the first part of my investigation. As to the result of the second part, I examined the papers in the case of John Smith, 1877, and found the documents in nature, form, and handwriting were so absolutely identical that there could be no possible doubt that they were by the same man who had written the incriminating documents in the 1896 case. This was too obvious to need any demonstration. When before the magistrate at Westminster I gave my evidence on both points: first, that to the best of my belief the handwriting in the incriminating documents of 1896 was Mr. Beck's handwriting, and in regard to those I have already admitted frankly that I was wrong, and I did so the moment it came to my knowledge. I very deeply regret the error in judgment. Secondly, I gave evidence to the effect that the incriminating documents in the 1877 case were beyond any doubt by the same man that wrote the incriminating documents in the 1896 case. I may add that in the 1877 case there was no proved specimen of John Smith's ordinary handwriting. Such a specimen would have been of the greatest value. During the proceedings I carefully followed the case and the evidence of every witness, and it seemed to me that every particle of the evidence strongly confirmed the opinions I had formed. There were 10 or 11 women who identified Mr. Beck as the man who had robbed them (I witnessed one of the identifications myself) some of whom swore that they saw Mr. Beck write these documents. There were the identifications by the two police officers of Mr. Beck as the man John Smith in their custody in 1877. There was the absolute identity of the writing in the 1877 and 1896 cases, and there was the fact that the late Mr. Inglis, my colleague, who was never loth to oppose me, had examined the documents on behalf of the defence, and he was not called to rebut my evidence, thus leaving me to assume that he shared my opinion. At the trial in 1896 my evidence as to the incriminating documents and Mr. Beck's handwriting was given. I expressed my conscientious opinion to the best of my belief. I never swear to handwriting, and in answer to Mr. Gill in cross-examination. I admitted, as I am always willing to do, the possibility of my being mistaken. I said I laid no claim to infallibility. The second part of my evidence, however, as to the identity of the 1877 and 1896 writings being identical, and which was manifest to anyone, was, I regret to say, not taken. At the trial in the present year I repeated the same evidence as in 1896, having, moreover, repeated to the Treasury that there could be no doubt that all the incriminating documents in 1877, 1896, and 1904 were written by one man. Had I then known that it had already been ascertained that John Smith and Mr.

Beck were two different persons, my report would
have been in Mr. Beck's favour, as to assume him
guilty under these circumstances would, on the handwriting, have been a contradiction. I was still
convinced that the John Smith of 1877 and Mr. Beck
were one. In July last, when Mr. Beck was still in
detention, I heard of the arrest of another man for the
same class of fraud, and of a letter said to be identical
with the writing in the incriminating documents in
the previous cases. I saw it on Sunday, the 17th July,
and was astounded to find the identical hand that had
been used in all the incriminating documents
throughout. Then for the first time I recognised that
Mr. Beck could not be John Smith. On Monday, the
18th, I went to Lord Desart and to the Chief
Commissioner of Police, and stated that in view of
that letter I was convinced of Mr. Beck's innocence.
In conclusion, I can only express my deepest sympa-
thy with Mr. Beck in his terrible trials, and my
heartfelt regret that his innocence of the charges
brought against him was not discovered in time to
spare him his many years of suffering.

Sir JOHN EDGE: I understand you to say that
the incriminating documents of 1877, the incriminating documents of 1895, and the incriminating
documents of 1904 are exactly in the same handwriting?—Absolutely identical in every respect.

No doubt could be entertained by anyone that
they were written by the same man?—Absolutely
impossible for there to be any question at all of
that.

Do you still think that that was a disguised hand? You see there was an interval of 27 years between 1877 and 1904. Do you think a man would carry on exactly the same character of disguised hand for 27 years?–I have to answer that in two ways; the last part of the question first. It is quite possible that a man may adhere to the same form of disguise for a large number of years.

What you mean by a disguised hand is that it is not his natural hand?–Not his natural hand.

But only used on particular occasions?–Yes, that is so.

You have it in 1877, and then you have it 18 years afterwards, in 1895, and again 27 years after the first, in 1904. Do you think that a man would carry forward the same peculiarities in disguising his hand during all those years and leave no trace of any difference?–It is, I think, quite manifest, on examining the incriminating documents, that some portions of them are intentionally disguised.

Put the signatures on one side. Take the bodies of the documents. Is there the slightest difference in the writing in all these years?–I may say that, take them all in all, the writings of 1877, 1896, and 1904 are manifestly by one hand, even including the differences which appear on the documents themselves. Sometimes the John Smith writing is a small writing, with a forward slope, and nothing like so distorted as at others. At other times it is a very large writing, written backwards, and apparently written right from the elbow, without apparently controlling the wrist. I can show in a moment, I believe, what I mean by referring to a tracing.

Really, what I was trying to come at was, whether you concluded that the incriminating documents in 1895 and 1896 were in a disguised hand, because the hand differed from Mr. Beck's ordinary hand?–No, those were not the grounds on which I concluded that it was disguised. It was the distortion, the irregularity of angle, and the difference of style in the incriminating documents themselves.

Then if you had seen none of the genuine writing of Mr. Beck at all, you would still have been of opinion that the documents of 1895 and 1896 were in a disguised hand?–Yes.

Sir SPENCER WALPOLE: The documents as well as signatures? Signatures are obviously, as you have described it, inverted?–There was other writing besides the signatures; for instance the bills of exchange and the addresses on the envelopes. For instance, here is a facsimile of writing taken from those incriminating documents (*documents produced*). Some of it is very large. These are upright, and backward, and small with the forward slope. All those handwritings were taken from the same set of documents.

Sir JOHN EDGE: Of course, I am not an expert?–It is the enormous difference in the style.

As a matter of fact, do you find there is any difference in the style of a man's writing over a period of 27 years?–It depends upon what period you compare them with.

I say over a period. Is it your opinion that a man's

writing remains the same for a period of 27 years?–It often does; sometimes it does not. I have seen writing written at an interval of 35 years. A woman's writing, compared when she was 25 with when she was 60, and the two signatures looked as if they might have been written almost at one sitting.

And the body of the letter?–I am only speaking of the signature.

Sir SPENCER WALPOLE: If you had known in December, 1895, that the marks on Beck's body did not correspond with the marks on Smith, would you have modified your opinion?–If I had known that there were marks that refuted his identity, certainly. I should have said it was impossible.

You were not informed of any such difference in marks by the police, were you?–I heard on one occasion, I think, that there was some discrepancy, something in the way of a mole or a wart, but it struck me that it was of such a nature that it might have been transient at the time, and that the lapse of years would have accounted for it disappearing.

If you had known in 1904 that there was a distinct difference between the marks in the two bodies, the one being a circumcised and the other an uncircumcised man, would that have modified your opinion?–I should say so, most decidedly, because I was absolutely conscious of the fact all the way through that it must have been the 1877 man that committed these frauds.

And, as a matter of fact, you did not receive that information? –No.

.

Sir JOHN EDGE: From the point of view of an expert, I suppose it would be immaterial that you should receive that information, would it not?–I take the greatest notice of facts.

Yes, but are not those outside facts likely to influence your judgment as an expert? I mean if you find there are ten or eleven witnesses who identify a man, would that strengthen your view that you were correct in your view of the writing, as an expert?–I think so, undoubtedly, if I heard ten or eleven witnesses declare a fact, and I believed their statement, it would certainly strengthen my opinion.

It would strengthen your opinion that you were correct in your criticism of the writing?–Yes, all the evidence that I heard from time to time did confirm me in the belief that my opinion was an accurate one.

Can you say that it did not influence your opinion when you were coming to a conclusion in this matter?–No, it did not influence me in the first place. Step by step it confirmed me.

The CHAIRMAN: Thank you, Mr. Gurrin.

The Witness withdrew.

Mr. ADOLF BECK: May I put a question to Mr. Gurrin with regard to Mr. Gurrin's statement.

The CHAIRMAN: Let me know what the question is.

Sir GEORGE LEWIS: The question is: Does Mr. Gurrin think that, if he had been allowed to give evidence at the trial and was not stopped from doing so, his evidence would have made Mr. Beck's innocence apparent at the trial.

The CHAIRMAN: He said so.

Mr. WILLIAM HAMILTON LEYCESTER, called
and Examined.

The CHAIRMAN: You are a Member of the Bar, and
I think you were Counsel for the defence in Mr.
Beck's last trial in 1904?–That was so, my Lord.

Were you alone?–I was alone.

Will you kindly tell us what you think material in
respect of that trial?–My Lord, I think that there really
is only one point upon which I can assist the
Committee, but it is one of some importance. At the
second trial you will see by referring to the Sessions
Papers that the allegation of Mr. Beck, which he had
made all through, that these offences were committed
by the man Smith, and that he was not Smith, was not
raised as his defence at all, and in fact the judge and the
jury who tried the case never heard any suggestion that
these offences had been committed by Smith, and the
case was treated by me as an ordinary case of alleged
mistaken identity and nothing more. That being so, as
I was the person who was solely responsible for that
line of defence being taken, and as it was done much
against Mr. Beck's will, I think I ought to explain to the
Committee why it was that I took that line. The facts
were these: Mr Beck at the police court was defended
by a solicitor named Mr. Freke Palmer. He was committed to take his trial at the Old Bailey Sessions,
which began on the 20th June–a Monday. Of course a
defence of this kind was one which required a great
deal of preparation. It required the presence of wit-

nesses from Sweden, and, for all I know, the presence of witnesses from South America, and it was one obviously which would involve a good deal of expense, and I suppose Mr. Freke Palmer realised that. Apparently the funds were not forthcoming, and Mr. Beck's defence had not been prepared.

You mean that part of the defence which rested on an *alibi*?–Yes, my Lord, that part of the defence which went to prove that he could not be Smith.

Only that part of the defence which rested upon the *alibi*. The argument from the handwriting in the letters and incriminating documents, and the argument from the precise similarity of the methods of the two persons, were still open and might have been adduced if thought desirable?–That would have shown that the offences were committed by Smith; it would not have shown that Beck was not Smith. It was no good doing one without doing the other.

That two persons as to whom there was no evidence on the part of the Crown that they had ever had any opportunity of collaborating, could, at an interval at 19 years, by a coincidence, hit, not only on the same device in particular as well as in principle, but should also carry it out in the same handwriting–surely those two coincidences would have been so extraordinary as to lead to the presumption that they were done by one and the same person?–That is so, my Lord, but they do not go to show that Mr. Beck was not that person.

Evidence of the alibi, no doubt, would be required for the next limb of the case?–The first step in the argument is of no use unless you are able to prove the second. It is no good saying that all the offences were committed by the same man unless you go on to show that Mr. Beck was not Smith.

Yes, you are quite right. Then there was no other evidence accessible upon the alibi, no other evidence of persons, in this country I mean?–There was no other evidence, as far as I know. There was, of course, the all important fact that one man was a circumcised Jew and the other was not, of which, for my part, I was absolutely ignorant. Upon the second day of the sittings, Mr. Freke Palmer had an application made to the court that the case should be postponed until the following Sessions. That application was opposed, and it was refused. The consequence was that Mr. Freke Palmer threw up the case. Mr. Beck was left with nobody representing him, and upon the next day, I think the 22nd June, his case was in the list. When it was called on, he himself made an appeal to the Recorder not to try the case that Sessions. He said he was unrepresented; he had no witnesses, and could not possibly conduct a case of that kind himself; and the Recorder granted the application, and postponed the case to the July sittings. But upon the next day, the 23rd June, Counsel for the Treasury made a third application that the case should come on forthwith, and they made that upon affidavit by a police officer that most of these women who were to give evidence against Mr. Beck were about to leave the country, and that if the case was not taken there would be, by the time the next Sessions arrived, only one available witness for the prosecution, and that she was at that time too ill to leave her bed, and the affidavit went on to state that there was no ground whatever to suppose that Mr. Beck would ever be in a financial condition to properly provide for his defence; that he would probably be in exactly the same position the next Sessions as he then was. The Recorder, upon that affidavit, did what I suppose he could not possibly help doing; he ordered that the case should come on. He told Mr. Beck that he must be prepared with his defence by the following Monday, which would be the 27th, and that the case would, upon that day, be first in the list. Mr. Freke Palmer having retired from the case, Mr. Williams, who, I understand, is an old friend of Mr. Beck, and who is a solicitor, took the case up. That would be on the Thursday or the Friday, and upon the Saturday he came down to the Temple and instructed me to appear for Mr. Beck. We were then in this position: that, as your Lordship has pointed out, we might possibly be able to prove that these offences were committed by Smith, but we had not a single witness to show that Smith and Beck were not identical.

The reason I put the question to you a moment ago is this. Certainly it seems to me that if you had been in a position–I am not suggesting, I need not say, anything like want of due care or diligence at the trial–but if you had made the point in the presence of the learned judge who tried the case, arising on the letters only, tending to show, at all events, very strong evidence for you that the person who committed these deeds must have been one and the same person, and had then told him that the prisoner desired to show, and you were instructed could show, and in point of fact at an earlier trial had produced witnesses to prove, that he could not have been the person who committed the earlier crimes, I am absolutely satisfied that the learned judge would have at any cost, post-poned the trial in order to make certain whether that evidence existed or not?–My Lord, I do not doubt that is so.

No application was made to him based on that? You did not go into the inference arising from the similarity of the letters?–No, my Lord.

And not having laid that foundation you could not make any real foundation for a postpone-ment?–No, my Lord.

No suggestion of the kind was made?–No, my Lord.

It never came out before the learned judge?–No, my Lord, he never heard a word of it. I think I ought to say this, that at the time the trial commenced, I myself did not know that, as it appears now, there could not have been any doubt that the documents of 1877 and the documents of 1896 and 1904 were all in the same handwriting.

You never had any opportunity of inspecting them?–I have not seen them to this moment. I ought to say that I really did not know that until after Mr. Gurrin had been in the box, when I spoke to Mr. Gurrin myself during the adjournment and asked him what the truth was about that. Mr. Gurrin, it is only fair to him to say, told me that there could be no opinion about it. It was not a question of opinion, but it was quite obvious to anybody who looked at them.

I think if you saw the documents you would agree?–My Lord, that probably is so. So that until the trial was half through, I did not really know even that that fact could be established–that the documents really were all in one handwriting.

The learned judge never had an opportunity of comparing them for himself?–I do not think he knew of their existence. That being so, if I had raised at that trial, in the circumstances in which I was, any question as to these offences being committed by Smith, the sole thing I could have done would be to bring out the fact that Mr. Beck had been committed in 1896, and that in all probability he had been convicted in 1877 as well, and I am afraid that would not have assisted him.

I fully appreciate the very certain dangers for the uncertain advantage?–Mr. Williams, I may say, had known Mr. Beck for some time. He was acquainted with the general facts of the case, but had never gone into it in detail, and there were a large number of facts, which I need not go into now, of which Mr. Williams was ignorant, and of which I was quite ignorant at the time the trial came on. The only opportunity I had of speaking to Mr. Beck was we had about 10 minutes conversation in the dock just before the trial came on. There were a number of things which were most important to his case, of which I had not been informed.

Mr. Williams gave evidence, I see, as to the handwriting of the incriminating documents not being the handwriting of Beck?–Yes, he was called in for that purpose. He was the only witness I had.

No evidence was given on the other point, that the handwriting of all the incriminating documents was the same?–No, my Lord, I did not know of any human being in existence who had seen them all, except Mr. Gurrin. My Lord, that being so, I felt that was the only defence I could raise for him, and I think so now in the circumstances in which I then was; but it was my decision; I am responsible for it, and I do not want to throw the responsibility in any way upon anybody else. Of course, the result was that, the case being taken under these circumstances, this man has been twice convicted, and his defence has never been heard by any jury. My Lord, there is only one other thing I should like to inform the court of, and that is, that the day after the trial I sent a message to Inspector Ward that I should like to see him, because it was quite clear to my mind that there was something extraordinary about this case.

That, of course, was after Mr. Beck had made his own statement?–Yes, my Lord.

In which he had referred again to the fact that he had been mistaken for a man named Smith?–Yes, a statement which was made in such a way that it very much impressed a great many people who heard it in court. Ward came up to see me, and gave me all the information which he then possessed, and, in justice to him, I should like to say, if I may, that the impression left upon my mind was that he was sincerely anxious to make any inquiries he could which would tend to clear up the case. I think he believed in Mr. Beck's guilt, but he realised that it was an exceptional case, and he said that if I could suggest anything to him he could do to clear it up, he would be only too pleased to do it, and I think he was sincere and honest in making that statement. I do not think, my Lord, that there is any other matter which occurs to me upon which I can assist the Committee. I have brought my brief here which I had from Mr. Williams, so that the Committee, if they cared to, could see what instructions I had at the time.

We are absolutely content, I need not say, with what you tell us now?—My Lord, might I say this? The first knowledge that I ever had from anybody that Smith was a circumcised Jew and Beck was not, was when Inspector Ward told me so, two days after Smith's arrest. He came up and saw me again, and told me what he had done, and he told me that fact.

The CHAIRMAN: We are much obliged to you.

The Witness withdrew.

Mr. Justice GRANTHAM, called and Examined.

The CHAIRMAN: You are here at your own instance?—Certainly, at my own instance in one sense, that some time ago I thought it was much better that my statement should be made in some way or other. Beyond that I have taken no steps to come here until I had a communication from you or your secretary, both, in fact, asking what my view was as to whether I should make a statement, and as I had in August written to the Home Office saying that I thought my statement ought to be made, I am here in accordance with your wish, for I thought it right that I should make a statement.

I daresay you have seen what happened when the learned Recorder was called. I have no doubt you agree with the general principle which we then stated?–I may say I have; and yet, perhaps, I ought to qualify that by saying that I have had a great many things on my mind in the last week or two, and I have not had time to read the whole of the evidence. I saw apparently a summary in the paper, not a very full account. I have not had time to read the evidence.

I am not suggesting evidence. I am merely referring to the principles which we laid down, and governing our right to hear anything about the matter?–Yes. I think the best course I can adopt is to read a letter, I do not know if there is anybody here representing the Home Office, but I think I have the permission of the Home Office to read a letter which I wrote to the Home Secretary in August.

The CHAIRMAN: Mr. Chalmers is there. I daresay he will give the authority if necessary.

Mr. CHALMERS : Certainly.

The WITNESS: I did not like to do it without authority. I wrote a letter in August to the Home Secretary. I think it is right that I should read that now, because that was written before I knew anything that has since come out, excepting the mere fact that it was quite clear that there had been a mistake made, and I thought, therefore, while the matter was fairly fresh in my mind it would be much better that I should communicate with the Home Office and put them in possession of all that I knew about it, in case they might be able to make use of it in any way they liked. Therefore, with your permission, I will read the letter: "Culachy, Fort Augustus, N.B. August 28th. Dear Home Secretary. Just before coming here my attention was called to a letter of mine in answer to one of a Mr. H. Furniss as to the Adolf Beck case, and from which it was inferred that I had been deceived by some person or persons to induce me to believe that Beck was guilty. Seeing very few but Scotch papers here, I do not know what, if anything, has taken place recently about the case, but as I do not like the impression to remain that I was deceived by anyone, and as I think you ought to know all that I know about the case, as it may assist you to some extent in case you hold a public inquiry, to allay the not unnatural sensitiveness of the public after such a miscarriage of justice as has just taken place, I will tell you exactly what happened at and after the trial. The case was not in the judge's list for trial at the Old Bailey, and I knew nothing of it till the last day of the Sessions, when there were only two causes left for trial"–if I might be allowed to add now, I should like to do so, that the statement made by Mr. Leycester is quite new to me; I never heard before as to the applications for postponement that he has mentioned–"viz.: this case of Beck and the case of the woman Watson, who was charged for perjury in alleging that General FitzHugh, a visiting justice of Lewes Prison, had promised her marriage. As Watson knew that General FitzHugh was a neighbour of mine, the Recorder suggested that he should try Watson and I should try Beck, especially as he said he had previously tried him for the same kind of offence and given him seven years' penal servitude, that after the trial Beck had petitioned the Home Office alleging he was not guilty, and had not been previously convicted, under the name of Smith, but that although Beck and Smith might not be the same person, yet after the Home Office inquiry the conviction before him stood, and Beck had served his full time as there was no doubt as to his guilt in the case that he had tried. As this exchange of prisoners was made almost at the last moment. I had not time to read the depositions before the trial. That the extraordinary frauds alleged by the prosecution had been committed by some one there was no doubt, and the identification of the prisoner by all the witnesses was equally clear, and as far as I could see, was irreproachable, but I could find nothing else to confirm the case for the prosecution, and as some of the frauds had been committed some time and the witnesses had not recently seen the prisoner, I was a little anxious lest they should have made a mistake in their identification. The evidence of similarity in handwriting was to my mind valueless and I told the jury so, for the handwriting of all the documents of the person committing the frauds was so manifestly feigned and

illegible that it was impossible to take any compar-
isons as a safe guide. No alibi could be raised, or what
was more important, tested, owing to the different
and uncertain dates the frauds had been committed,
and the period that had elapsed since some of them
were committed. The prisoner, of course, denied the
charge, but as at least 90 per cent. of the prisoners
who give evidence on their own behalf perjure themselves in denying the charge, the mere denial does not
have much weight, and unfortunately there was nothing that I could find out that was alleged on the
prisoner's behalf that made it impossible for him to
have committed the frauds alleged against him. His
position seemed peculiar. One thing in particular
struck me, namely, that, though it was alleged his
solicitor was paying him a certain sum per week, yet
he had not for some time paid the restaurant keeper
for his board. I have such implicit faith, from my long
judicial work, in the accuracy of the Home Office
inquiries and in the way they give ear to and sift
everything that can be found out that will help the
prisoner, quite apart from laws of evidence by which
judges are limited and sometimes hampered in public
trials, that I, of course, took it for granted, as the
Home Office had investigated the case and the conviction was confirmed, that he had been guilty of
some frauds before, and apparently of a somewhat
similar nature, though of the details I knew nothing,
nor of the character of the frauds committed by
Smith in 1876; for I did not think it fair to the prisoner to let my mind be prejudiced against him by his

former misdeeds under these circumstances. And as his counsel, after a searching cross-examination, had failed to break down the identification of the witnesses for the prosecution, I thought I should not be justified in telling the jury to disbelieve the witnesses who had so positively identified him, and the jury thereupon found him guilty. Still, though I can hardly explain to you why, I was not satisfied in my own mind. I was convinced that the prisoner did not belong to the criminal classes, but the evidence taken together, both for and against him, seemed to point to the conclusion that he had a mania for duping these foolish women who were so easily gulled by the promise and prospect of fine silks, satins and jewellery. In the hope, however, of finding out something more about the case favourable to the prisoner, I said I should postpone sentence, a very rare occurrence for me, and directed him to be removed, and I adopted the unusual course of asking the counsel for the prosecution and for the prisoner to come to me and discuss the case with me. I told them at once what the impression on my mind was, and, at the most, I should only give a sentence of imprisonment for some months, that owing to his previous conviction and sentence I should probably make it twelve months. I may not have mentioned the amount at the time, but that was my intention; and also I told them of the uncertainty in my mind as to the case, but failed to find from our discussion anything which justified my uncertainty As they left me, the counsel for the prisoner, as well as, I think, for the prosecution, asked me to inquire into his state of mind, and I accordingly sent a request for the prison doctor to attend me the next day, at the Royal Courts of Justice, where and when I was returning for my ordinary judicial duties. I need not say I had heard nothing of the character of the previous investigation by the Home Office, much less of the discovery that Smith was a Jew, and that Mr. Beck was not; I only knew that he had served his full sentence after the Home Office inquiry. Strange as it may seem, I was still unhappy in my mind about the case, and so after thinking over what more I could do, I sent a special message to the Central Criminal Court to direct the detectives to come and see me at the Royal Courts of Justice. The doctor came. He assured me the man was perfectly right in his mind. Then the detectives came and I examined them as to the methods of the identification by the witnesses. I think there were five—and then as to their characters; and their apparent reliability—every answer seemed satisfactory, and closed the door at last to that undefined doubt I had in my mind, and I definitely settled what sentence I should pass; but to keep open the door as long as possible, I advisedly did not notify the sentence to the officials at the Old Bailey till the last moment, when I was leaving or had left for circuit" which was the 6th July if I remember aright. "Most fortunately for Mr. Beck, before the next Sessions at the Old Bailey came on, the original Smith was, I understand, caught, and the mistake that had been made was discovered, so that my intended sentence was never passed. To the best of my recollection the above is an accurate account of what took place before me. Yours faithfully.–Wm. Grantham." That was the statement which I wrote at the time. I think, perhaps, I ought to say that, I think I wrote a letter to the Home Secretary before, asking how it was that I had not had some communication made to me as to the history of the previous conviction of Smith and Beck, but Mr. Douglas said that he did not know personally anything about it, and he thought the Home Office did not either. It was nothing very important.

You are referring to your conversation with the Recorder?–No, I am referring to a letter. I say before this I believe I had written a letter to the Home Secretary more in the nature of a private letter, to ask how it was I had not been informed that Smith and Beck were two different people, because I had seen something in the paper about an Inquiry having been made by the Home Office; I was naturally rather annoyed, and I think I did write to Mr. Douglas to ask how it was that I had not been informed of it, but it was more a private letter than anything else. He simply said the matter should be inquired into, but that he personally was not able to give any information. I should just like to supplement the letter I have read by comments which will really explain a little more some matters which might be in doubts. The first point I think I ought to refer to is this. I am not certain whether the Recorder spoke to me himself about my trying the case, or whether he sent a message when I was at the Old Bailey. My impression now is, he sent a message to ask whether I would mind taking this case as he had heard that Watson rather objected to my trying her. I had tried the case of the alleged breach of promise, and I felt it my duty, as far as I could, to protect General FitzHugh from the vile charge which had been made against him, which fortunately did not depend so much on his evidence as on that of Colonel Isaacson, the governor of Lewes gaol, who is one of the most efficient public servants we have, and who has been twice promoted since. I thought it my duty to see that General FitzHugh was properly protected with regard to this extraordinary vile charge which had been made against him; and, therefore, although I knew that Watson had said I ought not to try the case, I thought it my duty to try it, and therefore I had not yielded to any of the suggestions made—although not publicly made—that I should not try it. However, when the Recorder sent a message to me to say that as he understood Mr. Beck objected to his trying the case again, would I mind taking it: I said, certainly. Of course your Lordship knows that judges only take the most serious cases, not misdemeanours of this kind; and therefore the depositions were not sent to me and would not be sent to me, and I knew nothing about the case until Mr. Beck was put into the dock, and I tried the case just as I would any ordinary case. It is a singular coincidence that I find the Recorder's letter which he sent to the "Times" is dated the 27th and mine is dated the 28th, but as his letter did not appear in the "Times" till the 29th, it is a proof that I had not seen it when I wrote to the Home Office because he was in England and I was in Scotland. I did not know of it until some considerable time afterwards when I came to England, and there had been no communication between us, although our letters were so nearly dated. There is not very much more to add, but I should like to say one or two things.

I should just like to ask you this upon that if it is convenient for you to answer it. After the interview with the Recorder was any doubt brought to your mind as to Smith and Beck being the same person?–The question was never raised. I don't think the name of Smith was ever mentioned.

Nothing had passed between you and the Recorder?–No, nothing at all. My impression is that the Recorder had never mentioned the case of Smith to me. I think I heard of it from Mr. Guy Stephenson, and that he told me that although Beck and Smith might not be the same person, yet after the Home Office inquiry the conviction stood, and he served his full time as there was no doubt of his guilt in the case which was tried. That enquiry certainly led me to believe there was no doubt whatever as to his guilt in that case. The next thing is the extraordinary frauds which had been alleged by the prosecution had been committed. I ought to say I used the expression "extraordinary frauds" not meaning the amount, but the character of the frauds. The next thing is as to the trial, and as to the evidence with regard to the handwriting. I have heard what Mr. Gurrin has said to-day. I need not go into the question at all as to the value of handwriting as evidence, but all I can say is that it was the fact of the prosecution relying on handwriting that made me hesitate as to whether or not they were right in the case. I may be wrong (I am only, of course, giving you what passed through my mind at the time) but to my mind it was absolutely impossible for anyone to rely on any assumed similarity of writing between that of Mr. Beck which they had, and that of the person who committed these frauds, and gave those extraordinary orders for dresses.

You were not able yourself to discover any *prima facie* resemblance between them?–I was certain that it was absolutely impossible to in any way say anything that was reliable, and I therefore told the jury straight, I have not any note of what I said, and I am only speaking from recollection, but my recollection of it is this: that I told them to discard the evidence altogether of handwriting; as it was not in any way reliable. It is only fair to Mr. Gurrin that I should add this. He has made a mistake in this case and he has frankly admitted it. I have known Mr. Gurrin for many years, and I have always found Mr. Gurrin very careful in previous cases, but I must say in this case I did think that having given evidence in 1896 or 1898, or whenever it was, and having come to a strong conclusion in that case, he was relying on a previously formed conclusion, and not on the facts of the particular case then before us. Then came the question–What was I to do? I searched in my mind in every way that I could to find something to corroborate the identification, and could find nothing. I have been at least twenty-five years judicially engaged in criminal trials. I have been on the Bench now nearly nineteen years, and before that I had five or six years' or more experience sitting as Chairman of Quarter Sessions, and I have never allowed a man to be convicted unless the evidence convinced me as well as the jury. I daresay some people may think I am wrong and that I ought to rely on the jury, but I have always adopted that principle and I have over and over again given considerable offence to Counsel by directing a jury to acquit a man when they thought the evidence was clear. I daresay they were quite right and I was quite wrong, but I have always acted on that principle. When I had, therefore, to determine what I was to do in the case, I had this uncertainty in my mind. These witnesses were positive, and according to them they could have made no mistake, but the question of identification depended on their accuracy and I knew from my experience, that it was possible people may be honestly mistaken, and I looked therefore for some evidence to justify the prosecution in saying it was a perfectly clear case. I looked through the handwriting, and failed to find such evidence, though the prosecution relied upon it That, in my judgement, weakened their case. Then I looked for something else—proof of any property found on him or anything connected with these people found on him; and I could find no corroboration of the case for the prosecution. We lawyers are always very fond of precedents, and if I may I will mention a case which I think will exemplify the difficulty I was in perhaps better than anything else I can say. It is a case the

President may probably remember, although he probably never knew the sequel It was a case I tried at Manchester where a somewhat similar question arose as to reliability of positive evidence for a prosecution. A warder was tried for practically the murder—it was called manslaughter—of a prisoner in the Manchester jail. There was a tremendous outcry about this. The papers were full of it weeks beforehand. I knew I was going down to Manchester, and should have to try him, so I would not read the papers about it. I read the depositions when I arrived. The depositions were clear. There was amongst other evidence the evidence of a fellow prisoner who in court graphically described the brutality exercised by this warder on the deceased man. The case was tried. I ought to tell you that the warder was a warder of the hospital ward of the prison, and in those days it was the custom for men charged with murder to be put in that ward. This warder had under his care, therefore, in this ward three men charged with murder, two of whom, if not three, I myself tried at that very assize. This fellow prisoner of the deceased man swore that this warder strapped the man on to a bed because he was under the influence of delirium tremens and kicked up a tremendous row, and he kneeled on him and broke his chest. He described the pummelling on his chest and his ribs, and, of course, there was a horrible feeling throughout the country. The doctor was called, who said that he found the man dead in his bed, and the injuries had been inflicted within five hours of the discovery that he was dead. The five hours coincided with the statement made by the fellow prisoner that that was when these injuries had been inflicted upon him. The case, therefore, was as clear as noonday apparently, but what was on the other side? There was the prisoner's denial which amounted to nothing but he had borne an exemplary character. He had been 12 years in the Army and left it with an admirable character; a first-class character. He had been two years in this very ward; which, if I may describe it in vulgar language, if there is a hell upon earth it was a ward like this, where there were people charged with murder, and people ill, and everything of that kind. Yet for those two years there was not a breath of suspicion that that man had ever been unkind. The feeling was so strong against him that the warders were afraid of getting up a subscription to have the man properly defended because it would be said if they did that they were in league with him. The result of it was he was only defended by a young man, who had a dock defence. The case was finished. There was not a loophole of escape. I myself helped the counsel, who was only a young man, and I failed, and the evidence could not be broken down. I said to myself, "What am I to do? I don't think the man did it." I then took every witness backwards, the last first, and so on, to the end. I did so, and they beat me again. I was face to face with the responsibility for the conviction of a man whom I did not think was guilty. What was I to do? I determined that I would back my opinion against the evidence, so I did not sum up the case at all. I turned to the jury and I said, "Gentlemen, if you believe that evidence you must convict the man of one of the most horrible crimes that has ever been committed, but if you trust me you will not." I said, "That man has been 12 years in the Army, and has left it with an exemplary character. He has been two years in that ward, and there is not a word against him. You may just as well tell me that a leopard could change her spots as that man could change his character in a night." That was my charge, and the jury turned round and said, "Not guilty." I need not say that I had a very hot and a very bad time of it for a long time afterwards. Of course, I do not blame people for abusing me. The press abused me, the Home Office abused me, and the House of Commons abused me. Mr. Bradlaugh, who was one of the most level-headed men ever in that House, took it up night after night, and the only thing he did not do was to move the House that I should be removed from my judicial seat. He did everything else, and I had letter after letter abusing me. I could only say "I have done the best. By our constitution you cannot go behind the judge, and I defy you to try that man again." I heard nothing more for a year, or, I think, it was two years when I went down to Manchester again and doing what I always do if I find time, which I am afraid is not very often on circuit, I went over the jail. The moment I rang the bell, and the porter saw I was coming, a message was sent to the Chief Constable, who came and told me what had been found out. He said, we found out afterwards that you were quite right, and that the evidence was quite wrong." The fact was that the man

had been subject to delirium tremens–and that the
injuries were inflicted before he was taken to prison
three or five days before, that the doctor had failed to
discover it at the time, and it was therefore more convenient, probably, to think that they had been
inflicted within five hours, and the fellow prisoner of
the man who was killed had worked up his evidence
accordingly, and the whole of his story was imagina-
tion, or nearly all of it. Now I had that case in my
mind when I had to determine what I should do in
reference to Beck, because I had these doubts. I could
find nothing to support the identification, but I
realised this. In the case I am telling you about I had
proof of good character of the warder, before me, and
I was able to act on my judgment, pinning my faith
to that. Could I do that in Mr. Beck's case? I thought
I could not, because I had the fact before me that he
had been previously convicted. Therefore I thought I
dare not do it, because it must be remembered in all
these cases you have got the character of the witnesses
for the prosecution to consider, and people often do
not realise that. Therefore, where I had the fact of
Beck's previous conviction before me I felt I was not
justified in discrediting these witnesses by telling the
Jury not to believe them.

Now I come to another part of the case, which
to my mind is unexplainable, and I am very glad to
have heard what Mr. Leycester has said here to-day,
because it explains what I could not understand until
this morning. I am not at all sure, in fact my belief is,
that if it had not been for what I am now going to tell

you I should have told the jury to acquit Mr. Beck. As Mr. Leycester has said, not a word was said about the previous trial or about any question of any difference in opinion as to whether Beck was Smith or Smith was Beck, or whether Beck was a Christian and the other a Jew, or anything of the kind, but I will just draw your attention to what made me think I was wrong in having any doubt about Beck's guilt. First of all there is the evidence of Stephen de Maria, coupled with what came out afterwards. Stephen de Maria, who was called for the prosecution, said: "Letters came to me for Mr. Beck. I allowed his letters to be addressed at my place. He said he was engaged in the City as a commission agent. He had breakfast at my restaurant and sometimes lunch, but not lately, and then he told me he was rather short. I said I have no objection. You can go on and pay me whenever you can. At present he owes me between £40 and £50." I thought at the time this is a funny thing when I heard Stephen de Maria's evidence, running up a score like this. It looked a little bit as if he were defrauding Stephen de Maria. The circumstances were, besides, peculiar. He did not sleep there; he breakfasted and dined there and slept somewhere else. It is not what English people, as a rule, do; at any rate they generally breakfast and dine where they sleep if they have not a home of their own. Afterwards when Mr. Williams gave his evidence I turned back to my notes to see what de Maria had said, and when I found that Mr. Williams (the solicitor) said: "I am engaged in the sale of property for him. I have the contract here. I made him an allowance because of that property, and because I had known him a long time and had respect for him. I should think I have given him £200, on an average £2 a week. There were no regular payments. I was prepared to lend him anything within reason"—when I heard that evidence I said to myself, That proves that Mr. Beck, I do not say was a cheat, but at any rate was getting breakfast and dinner out of this poor man, Stephen de Maria, under false pretences, because here he is getting money, and why does he not go and pay him? That was one of the things that influenced my mind when I at last determined to let the case go to the jury. Then Mr. Williams was cross-examined by Mr. Guy Stephenson, and he says: "I have a list of my payments. I have no receipts, except the cheques. Towards the end of last year I received £200 for the prisoner, which was part of £500 paid on his property." All that looked to me so extraordinary—that Mr. Beck should be living in this house in the way he was and getting his meals there, beginning by paying and then not paying anything although he was getting this money week after week from his solicitors. But it did not rest there. Not only did Stephen de Maria say that, but William Green, who is the manager of the Central Hotel, Percy Street, who knew the prisoner as Adolf Beck, said: "He stayed with me. When he left he owed me 39s." I thought that also most extraordinary when I found, according to this gentleman, Mr. Williams, that he had this money, and I must say that it affected my mind a good deal with regard to it. Then I pass on from that portion of my letter which alludes to the doubts I had. I then refer to another part of the case, as shown by the defence, which I must say impressed me very unfavourably with regard to Mr. Beck. Here was a solicitor who appeared for him and had known him a considerable time. Why in the world was it that there was not a more regular defence got up? Why was it that Mr. Palmer had left the case and was not able to continue it? Mr. Williams says this in the beginning of his evidence: "I am a solicitor. I have known the prisoner for 15 years. I have taken up his defence during the last week only." Then the whole of his evidence is as to handwriting, not as to his character. It is quite true he refers to it afterwards to a certain extent, but says nothing as to what he had known of him during those fifteen years, and he at once goes into the question of handwriting, and apparently he is only called to disprove the evidence of Mr. Gurrin, and that impressed me. I thought that was strange, especially when no witnesses to character were called.

You were not aware, were you, that there was a previous conviction at that time?—Yes, because I think the prisoner had given his evidence before this statement, and I had been told of the previous trial by the Recorder,

With regard to character, it would be rather difficult, in view of the previous convictions?—I am going to say a word with regard to that. The extraordinary thing was that the defence should have been got up in that way. He says: "I have only taken up his defence during the last week." I thought if he had known him for 15 years he would not have allowed him to be taken before the Old Bailey and merely take it up in this way, because apparently nobody else was doing it. Then came the evidence of Mr. Beck himself. He said that he did not know the women, and he had never seen them; he was in the City doing business and he was with a Mr. Gajardo all day in business, that he been mistaken for a man named Smith, his double, and that he was receiving £3 or £4 a week from Mr. Williams. (Mr. Williams said £2 a week on an average). He said he was receiving £3 or £4 a week, and I was surprised that he had not paid these people if he was receiving that amount. With regard to this statement that he had been mistaken for a man named Smith as his double, my impression is that I had never heard of Smith's name at that time at all in connection with this case, and it was just like any other case that might be brought up from the streets—a man charged and brought before me to try as if he had never been convicted before, although I knew the fact that he had been previously convicted. On this evidence I allowed Mr. Beck to be convicted, but I was fully convinced that Mr. Beck was not a criminal in the ordinary sense of the word. I knew that the Recorder took a different view, and from the evidence before him probably he was justified in taking that view. I am responsible, of course, only for what comes before me, and I felt in the greatest difficulty to determine what I ought to do, because knowing that others had taken a different view I was anxious to have some justification for my doubts. I thought that it was possible there might have been a mistake as to his identification, because he had been convicted before and so the witnesses might stick to it that he was the man. In order that he should not know there was any doubt in my mind, I sent Beck away from the dock so that he should not know what I was doing, and I asked Mr. Guy Stephenson and Mr. Leycester to come and see me, which they did; and the former frankly said that he believed Beck was Smith. He referred me to the Sessions Papers report of Smith's trial to show that they must have been the same man. Mr. Leycester, who appeared for Mr. Beck, could not give me any further information. Mr. Leycester told me all he could, which as he told you to-day was very little; but there was one thing said which confirmed the view that I had taken that this was a mania if he were guilty. I think it was Mr. Leycester who said it, it was, "Will you inquire into his state of mind?" I thought "Then Mr. Leycester thinks that he is guilty and he has taken the same view I have as to his state of mind." At any rate it was the view apparently of both of them that it was worth while that I should enquire as to his state of mind; and therefore before leaving the court that day I there and then ordered someone to communicate with Dr. Scott and ask him to come and see me at the Law Courts. There was an end of the case as far as I was concerned at that time. It was the last case at the Old Bailey and I left. As I walked home I was still unhappy about the case, and I thought, "What can I do to find out if there is anything more behind it?" So when I got to my own private house I sent a letter to the Central Criminal Court requesting the authorities there to communicate with the police who had given evidence—to come and see me at the Law Courts. They came; and I think it is only fair to the police to say this, I have had a very great experience in evidence given by policemen, and, with very few exceptions, I have found them very fair; and whenever I have talked to them privately about cases I have never found them, in the whole of my experience, trying to get a man convicted, or doing anything which would prejudice the prisoner. It may be that I was not justified in relying on what might be called evidence for the prosecution, but I went to them on behalf of the prisoner. I examined them as carefully as I could, as to the method of their identification and as to the character of the women; whether they thought that they were reliable; whether they were prejudiced; or whether the fact if they knew it that he had been previously convicted had any impression upon them or affected their minds at all. I asked them about Mr. Williams. I asked if they could explain in any way the payments made by Mr. Williams to Mr. Beck, and his not paying the hotel keepers. I asked about his property. I asked if they had found out anything about that but I could find nothing that was favourable to the defence. I did not go into the other matter of the previous conviction because I knew the more I went into it, the worse it would be for Mr. Beck. I had not a suspicion as to what has come out since as to the mistake in the evidence as to the identity of Smith and Beck. Under those circumstances, after I had had this long conversation with the detectives, I came to the conclusion that nothing more could be done, and that I must allow the conviction to stand as it was, and I must pass sentence. The next incident was that some time afterwards, not long of course, because I went on circuit on the 6th July. I had a letter from a Mr. Furniss. I did not know him. We very often have letters from a prisoner's friends and they often write extra-ordinary letters without the slightest foundation for them. Sometimes they are civil and sometimes not. Sometimes I acknowledge them, if I think they ought to be (*i.e.*, my clerk does), but this letter of Mr. Furniss's was evidently the letter of a gentleman, and I therefore answered it myself. I must say that when I heard afterwards, and have heard since, of course, all that had taken place during the years 1894, 1895, 1896–the trial, I think, was in 1896–1897, and 1898, and all these persistent applications to the Home Office very properly made by Mr. Beck, and the firm view his friends had that he was innocent, I think I have a right to complain that as a judge I was not helped in the inquiry that I was making, and I was allowed to grope about in the dark, as I was, being on the scent of something having gone wrong, and never having any help in the matter from his friends. Why in the world they did not retain Mr. Gill, I do not know. Here was £200 at least in the hands of his solicitor, and he paid him £3 or £4 a week, Mr. Beck says. Mr. Gill had been fighting for him before, and believed it was a wrong conviction. Anybody who knows the position of Mr. Gill, and anybody who knows me, I hope, knows that any counsel, however junior he may be, if he had merely hinted in court that there was a chance of something wrong–and told me there were any of these difficulties, the whole thing would have been out; and I must say I do feel a good deal hurt that I had been allowed to grope about in the dark, and then that all this should come up, and the whole thing be exposed as clearly as possible. I apologise if I have said more than I ought to, but it is very difficult for a judge in the position I am placed in here to-day to know how much to say, and I have thought therefore, that the only course I could adopt was to tell you everything that was passing through my mind, because it is by thought and not by law that you have to determine whether a man is guilty or not. It is not the principles of law which will tell you whether a man is telling you the truth, it is by constant experience and arguing the thing in one's mind while the evidence is being given and the case is going on, that you are able to form correct conclusions. I think that is all, my Lord, that I have to say. I am very willing to answer any questions.

The CHAIRMAN: There is only one question I should like to put to you. I think you have already practically answered it. If you had been told that it was conclusively proved that Beck was not Smith, would it have been any different in your view of this case?–The question answers itself. There cannot be a doubt; it would have altered my view. The fraud was of such a peculiar character that it was almost impossible that two different people could have committed exactly the same fraud, and therefore if I had the slightest suspicion that there was anybody else, or might have been anybody else, previously convicted of the same offence, the matter would have been fully investigated at once.

You do not regard the issue whether Beck was Smith as an immaterial issue?–It is the most material issue in the case, to my mind.

Sir JOHN EDGE: Who could have given you the information that it had been proved that Smith and Beck were not the same man?–Of course, in one sense, that is where the difficulty may come in, but then in my opinion–it is only a matter of judgment–I think the case ought to have been fought on that issue; it should have been faced at once. Now that I know all that has taken place, by the constant petitions of Mr. Beck to the Home Office, and the certainty that he was in the right and that the other people were in the wrong, I cannot understand how those who were advising him did not face the difficulty at once, and admit the previous conviction, but challenge its justice.

You know, I presume, that the Home Office knew nothing of the 1904 Beck case until Smith was arrested, after Beck had been convicted?–My answer, of course, was more not as to what the prosecution should or should not have done, but as to the way in which the case should have been fought by the prisoner: that the difficulty of the fact of the previous conviction should have been faced by his advisers at once so that the matter could be brought out. It seemed to me incredible that with all the knowledge they had, Mr. Gill himself was not instructed, or as I have said before it would have made no difference, if anyone else had appeared before me, but it would have added so much to the strength of the application if Mr. Gill himself was brought there; but if any counsel had said: "My Lord, this man has been previously convicted of a similar offence, but although it has been investigated by the Home Office there have been matters brought out which to our mind show that that conviction was wrong and we must ask you to let us say what they are," I should at once have consented, but supposing I had said, "No, I cannot while the trial is progressing"; the moment the man had been convicted I should have said, "What is the meaning of all this that you tell me?" and I should have asked the counsel to come to me; and I should have had all the history of the case out and dealt with it as the facts required.

The CHAIRMAN: We are much obliged to you.

Mr. BECK: May I state that the most part of the £600 which I received during the 34 months when I was free was used for my investigations in coming to the truth of this matter. It was therefore in the latter part that I had to ask Mr. de Maria to help me with a little credit I received altogether £900 during the time. I received £500 as an option for working my copper property, out of which I had to provide £300 for expenditure which has been going on on the property.

The WITNESS: Of course I knew nothing of that. It was something not mentioned to me at all.

The Witness withdrew.

The SECRETARY read the following statement of Mr. Beck;–

"I was born in Christiansund, Norway, on the 14th January, 1841. My father was a merchant captain and a merchant. I was educated in Christiansund up to the age of 16 years, when I was put into a merchant's office. Office life did not suit me. I wished to go to sea, but my father objected, and I then entered the establishment of a scientific chemist to study chemistry. After a time I did go to sea for a year, then I came to England, arriving at Cardiff in 1865 or 1866. I went to Bristol to improve my English and entered an office as water clerk to a ship broker, and I went to Cardiff, Liverpool, Falmouth, Aberdeen, and Glasgow. I left Glasgow at the end of 1868 for South America, arriving at Monte Video, where I remained nearly a year. I there met Mr. Gottschalk the pianist. I was then a singer and I used to sing with him to the best people at Monte Video. I then came across a gentleman who asked me if I would undertake the business of cutting bank notes, that is, dividing notes which used to arrive in books from America. These notes were extremely numerous, ranging in value from 1s. to 1,000 dollars. I had to find a guarantee of 10,000 dollars. I remained in this employment for nearly six months; then I took to brokering, selling and buying shares, houses, and other property. The revolution broke out in which I fought, and I still have on my right arm a big scar made by a sword wound. Mr. Gottschalk then telegraphed me from Buenos Ayres and I joined him there and stayed a year in a shipbroker's office. I then went to Paraguay with merchandise for sale, had the fever there, and got back to Rosario and then to Cordova and went up the mountains for two months. The Minister of the Interior, with whom I was on terms of friendship, gave me employment on the Exhibition as manager of the outside works and to keep the time of about 3,000 men. I stayed there only two years and then went to Chili. From Chili I went to Bolivia to the silver mines and remained there two years mining. I came back to the port and formed a company to build a theatre. I afterwards went to Iquita and met Colonel North and we went together to his nitrate property to look for petroleum but without success. I then went to Lima in the beginning of 1874 and remained there until 1884 doing broking business, buying and selling houses, shares, &c. I afterwards went up to Iquita for a few months and got another concession. With this concession. I took a partner, Count Tronchet, who deceived me, and I had to get rid of him in Panama. The documents relating to these transactions are all in my possession. I left Panama during the Revolution time and went to Colon and had to wait ten days for a steamer. From there I went to New York and had an interview with a son of General Grant, who took my concession over to his father. General Grant told me I should have great difficulty with it, and it fell through. I came to London in May, 1885, and went to the Covent Garden Hotel. I had a letter of recommendation to Messrs. Attolla Bros. to take up my concession, but they said they could not do with it. I went to the Colonial Office, and there they could not do anything with it for the moment. I then intended going back to South America, but I happened to meet a Spaniard who had a concession for a railway in Spain, and I took this to Attolla Brothers, and they took it up, and a fortnight, afterwards they bought it for £32,000 my commission being £15,000, but all I received was £8,000. The capitalisation of the company was £1,200,000, and in case that was raised there would be a commission on that. I handed over the same firm a dock to be built by the concession which they took up, and my commission was £4,000, but I never received anything further. The £8,000 was paid to me in different sums. With £4,000 I went to Norway and bought copper property, part of which I still hold. Some of the lodes in the property I have lost owing to my imprisonment. Then I went into several businesses, selling and buying shares and other matters, and made a little money. I borrowed from Brown of Covent Garden Hotel £900 in 1893 or 1894 when I was in low water, copper being low. In the latter part of 1894 I became acquainted with Mr. Baker, of Baker and Jenkins, of Fenchurch Street, now of 3, Princes Street, Bank. I brought to them Hannan's Main Reef, for which I got £500 in cash and £4,000 in shares. Then I introduced some African property to them, for which I was offered £5,000 in shares; but owing to my imprisonment I lost that. I met Mr. Godfrey Chadwick, manager of the West End branch of an American insurance company, and he took up my copper property; also a patent lock, and during the time I was in prison he floated it, and he has been living on it the whole time I was in prison, and I have got nothing out of it. I left Covent Garden Hotel in the latter part of 1893, and went to Buckingham Hotel, Strand, for $2\frac{1}{2}$ years. Then I took a flat 139, Victoria Street, Westminster. I have never been convicted in any country except in England. On the 16th December, 1895, I was standing at my door, watching for a newspaper boy when a woman came up and said "What have you done with my watch?" I said, "Madam, I do not know you, you are mistaken." She said, "Oh no, I am not mistaken." I said, "If you do not go away I shall give you in custody." She annoyed me a little more, and I said, "Come with me." I walked with her to the first policeman, and said, "This woman is annoying me, making false accusations, and I beg of you to take her up." He said, "You must come too." I said, "Certainly." He went to the Police Station and I said to the inspector, "This woman has been annoying me; I give her into charge for making a false accusation." She said, "He has stolen from me a watch and some money." The inspector took her statement, but he did not take mine, and they detained me instead of her. I had not been there five minutes before two other

women came in and said, "Yes, that is the man." I said,
"I have never seen these women in my life before." I
was locked up. The next morning I asked the policeman to go to my friend Mrs. Millet, and also Mr.
Baker for them to come and see me. The policeman
came back and said, "I have seen the lady, and Mr.
Baker is not in town, but I have recommended Mr.
Dutton to her. I am a Cornish man and Mr. Dutton
is a very good man." Mr. Dutton appeared in Court
for me when the women gave evidence and I was
remanded. I was placed amongst some other men in
the yard for identification. I wore a high hat and
always stood at the end. Two other women came and
identified me. I was remanded to Holloway Prison. At
Holloway Prison I was stripped naked and my body
thoroughly examined and a full description of me was
entered in a book. On the second remand Inspector
Waldock took me into a room and stripped me to the
waist, and looked over my body, referring every
moment to a large book which he had on the table.
This book contained, I believe, the marks of John
Smith, of whom I had never heard. He showed me a
photograph of a good looking young man, and said,
"Do you know who that is?" I said, "I do not know
him." He smiled at this, and clearly led me to think it
was a photograph of myself. I was again put amongst
some men, and a woman came and stood there, and
was asked, "Can you see the man?" She said, No: I
believe it is that man standing there." "Well, put your
finger on him," said the policeman, but she would
not. He then took her umbrella and almost put it on

me. I was brought before the magistrate three or four times and committed for trial. A number of about twelve women said I was not the man. They had the same cheques in their possession and had been similarly defrauded, but the Police did not produce them or give to my solicitor or to me their names and addresses to enable me to do so, which I think is very unfair and not just. One day there were a lot of women in the yard and apart from six who said I was the man there were at least twelve who said I was not. Some said the other man was much darker, that I was not so tall, and he was stouter than me. Mrs. Townsend said in Court she heard me speak to Mr. Dutton and that my voice was quite different to that of the man she had been speaking of. When I was committed for trial I wished to speak on my own behalf but my solicitor advised me strongly not to do so. On the last remand at the Police Court, Mr. Gurrin, the handwriting expert, was examined and swore that the documents in the case were in the same handwriting as those of the man named Smith. He swore that the handwriting was the same as in 1877, and that the man who had written the documents in 1877 was the man who had written similar documents in 1895, and that the handwriting was identical. Police Constable Spurrell was examined at the last moment and he swore beyond a shadow of doubt that I was the man he arrested in 1877 and who gave the name of John Smith, and who told the woman he was Lord Willoughby, who gave cheques and got rings out of them, and that the crime was exactly the same as mine. The trial came on in March, 1896. My defence was that I was an innocent man and that the crime had been committed by John Smith and not by me; that the frauds were so identical in all respects that Smith, who was guilty of these frauds in 1877, could be the only person who could have committed the frauds of which I was accused. My defence was supported by the evidence of Mr. Gurrin, who swore that the documents supposed to be written by me were in the handwriting of John Smith. When Mr. Gill tried to raise my defence and to point out the identical circumstances of the 1877 frauds and to refer to Mr. Gurrin's evidence, counsel for the prosecution, without any apparent reason, withdrew the previous conviction and objected to any reference being made to it, and was supported by the Judge who ruled that Mr. Gurrin should not be asked the question of any reference made to the circumstances connected with Smith's crime in 1877. I was unable to be examined as a witness because the law did not enable me to do so and under such circumstances I was reduced to helplessness and was convicted. The Judge refused my counsel's request to state a case whether he was right in excluding the evidence and I was told that this being refused there was no Court to which I could appeal, as a matter of right, and I could only send in a petition to the Home Office. Also that there was no Court of Appeal in a criminal case as there is in my country. I, an innocent man, was according to the law in England, sent to seven years penal servitude without any appeal. My only hope lay in the Home Office, but I received no help from them and I suffered my imprisonment. There was a little woman, one of the witnesses, and another woman who said the man had a scar on his lower jaw, a large visible scar. The Judge ordered this woman to look at my jaw. The little woman came up (I think her name was Brilsford) to me in the box and I showed her my neck and she said "I cannot see the scar." Then the Judge ordered the warder to look, and he said "No, my Lord, there is no scar." Then he ordered the other woman to look, and she looked in front of the dock and pointed, and said "I believe it looks like a scar there." I stood with my neck exposed to Mr. Gill all the time that he might see that there was no scar." Then the Judge ordered the warder on my right side to look and told him to come into the witness-box, and he asked him if he saw any scar, and he said, "Yes, my Lord, it looks like a scar there." My counsel and my solicitor did nothing, although I was protesting I had got no scar. If the Judge or my advisers had asked a doctor to examine my neck, the falsity of the woman's statement would at once have been apparent. I was convicted and sentenced to seven years' penal servitude. I first went to Wormwood Scrubs and then to Chelmsford for eight months, then to Portland. I cannot remember when the letters D. W. were put on my clothing, but it was before I went to Portland. I did not know what they meant. After I had been in Portland about two months. I was told that they meant "previously convicted." Before going to Portland I sent a petition to the Home

Office. The first petition I wrote from Chelmsford I sent to the Home Office myself. I said I was absolutely innocent and a full statement of where I was in 1877. When I heard at Portland what D.W. meant I told the Governor that I had never been convicted before in my life. I sent in altogether 14 or 15 petitions, in all of which I protested my innocence and that I had never been previously convicted. I wish those petitions produced. The first answer I received was "No ground," then came "Not sufficient ground," and then came "Not quite sufficient ground." About two years after I had been in prison some one told me that John Smith was a Jew and that I ought to bring this fact before the Home Office. I did so and asked to be examined. A fortnight after I was examined by the Medical Officer and a fortnight after that Mr. Dutton came down and I told him. I showed him my arm, and he said "That is not the scar Smith had." It is true that John Smith has a scar on his right arm but it is quite an in-significant one. After Mr. Dutton had gone the Governor called me up and said "Your marks are changed from D.W. 533 to W. 78," and that he had been ordered by the Home Office to do so. I said "This is very strange if I am acknowledged not to be the man who was arrested in 1877 then they acknowledge the whole of my innocence." He said "That has nothing to do with me." I never knew and don't know now who identified me in prison or what inquiry was made to ascertain if the identification was true. I again petitioned the Home Office. I heard that copper went up in price and I went to the Governor and asked to be allowed to see another solicitor as I was allowed by the regulations to do so. They refused it. I asked several times to see a solicitor, but was always refused. I served out my sentence but served really longer than I ought to have done because at the last there was a conspiracy against me in prison. I was several times punished for talking and other trivial things. I was falsely accused several times, and got eight days bread and water. On the last occasion the doctor interfered, and said they would kill me if they went on like that, and I got full diet. I was employed in the tailors' shop and also in stonebreaking. I came out of prison in July, 1901. The Reverend Mr. Jackson, from Whitechapel, came to see me on my release, and I stopped with him until October, 1902, namely, 15 months. I went to Norway, and on my return stayed at the Central Hotel, Percy Street, Tottenham Court Road. I was there told to leave in consequence of Inspector Ward having called and told the proprietor that I had been up to my old tricks as in 1877 and 1896. When I came out of prison I tried to prove my innocence. I went to Mr. Dutton and asked him if he would go with me to the Home Office and explain the matter. I then saw Inspector Waldock and asked him if he could clear me. He said, "No, I cannot, and you will never clear yourself." I have heard that Mrs. Gardiner is a notorious woman who has been in prison. It took me a long time to find Mrs. Townsend. I found her out, but I told her servant an old acquaintance wanted to see her and would call to-morrow evening. I went the next

evening with Major Beasley, of the Salvation Army. I
asked Mrs. Townsend if she remembered me; she said,
"No." I said, "Have a good look at me," but she did
not know me. I said, "I have a particular friend of
mine who has been suffering $5\frac{1}{2}$ years in prison on
your statement." She said, "Who do you mean?" I
said, "A particular friend of mine, his name is Adolf
Beck." She said, "You mean the man who robbed me.
I said at the time I was not sure he was the man. I told
that to the police." Major Beasley asked her if she
thought she would know Adolf Beck again, and she
said, "Yes." I then invited her to dine with me, and we
went to a restaurant in Oxford Street, and I asked her
to tell me frankly what the police had said to her. She
said, "We were almost forced to," and then she
checked herself. She said, "Well you see there were
lots of women who said he was not the man." She
asked me for 30s. to help her pay a bill. I gave her that
sum and sent her home. About a week afterwards
Major Beasley and I took to her a statement of what
she had said and asked her to sign it, but she refused.
She said that detectives had been there, and said if she
said anything they would make it hot for her. I then
told her I was Mr. Beck, and she was surprised and
said she should not have dreamed it, and then said she
thought she recollected seeing me at the Court. I saw
Miss Meissonier who said I was the man right
enough. I saw the big woman but could not get anything out of her, and another woman I saw denied
being in the case at all, although I am sure she was. I
saw Sergeant Spurrell at Peter Robinson's and asked

him how he was. He said I had the advantage of him. I told him to look well at me, and he said: "Really, I do not know you." I said: "You had such a good memory before." I went back with a solicitor named Churchman, but Spurrell would not say anything. I got £5 from Mr. Dutton, then £250 from home, and £30 afterwards, £500 for option money on my property, out of which I paid £300, which was due. Then £200 from Mr. Williams, the solicitor, £50 from Maria. Altogether about £650 to live upon for 34 months. I received at the Central Hotel an anonymous letter in January, 1904, from a woman to be careful as they were going to get the same thing up against me as in 1896. I threw it in the fire. I heard nothing until Easter Sunday, April 3rd, 1904, when I was told by the servant of the hotel that the Proprietor wished to see me and they then told me that a detective and a woman were there and had said something. Early next morning, Easter Monday, I was told to leave the hotel. I got lodgings at 9, South Crescent. I went down to Maria and asked him to go with me to the Police Station. He said that there was someone there a week or a fortnight ago who gave his card as Inspector Ward. We went to Tottenham Court Road to see him, but they sent us to Walham Green Police Station, but we did not find him. I asked if I was wanted and they said no. I gave them my address 35, Oxford Street. On the 15th April I saw three people standing at the corner near my house, and one of them, a woman, came over to me and said, "I know you." I said, "I do not know you." She said,

"Yes, you took a sovereign from me." I said, "Who sent you here, the police? Now, look here, if you have a heart you know you are telling a lie, you know perfectly well I never stole from you, but I want to know who sent you. I am going to have my breakfast, come and tell me the whole story." She said "No, I have two detectives." Ward then came up and said, "We want you, do you know this man?" She said "Yes." He said, "Come with me." I said, "This is a bogus business; this is a got up affair amongst you, and you know it." He said, "We know what you are," and gave me to understand I had done the same thing before. I was taken to the station, and women were brought in and identified me the same day. Mr. Freke Palmer defended me first, but he gave it up for want of funds, and then Mr. Williams took it up at two days' notice. I was defended at the trial by Mr. Leycester. I was brought up before Sir Forrest Fulton, and he was asked to postpone my case till next Session. He refused. The next day I was brought up again, and I made a speech to Sir Forrest Fulton and showed it was impossible for me to defend myself that day, and he granted postponement to next Sessions. Then the Police applied to Sir Forest Fulton that two German women had waited a week and wanted to give their evidence as they were going away, so Sir Forrest Fulton called me up again and said the case must be tried at once because of these women, but ultimately he gave me until the next Monday. I was tried by Mr. Justice Grantham. Mr. Gurrin was a witness, and swore that the documents were in the same handwriting as the writing in my pocket-book, and I was convicted, but sentence was postponed. I told Mr. Williams I wanted to go into the witness-box and tell the whole story of John Smith, but they would not let me. The Clerk of the court said I had been formerly convicted, I began to speak and said that in my defence I was innocent then as I am innocent now, and it stopped the Judge, who postponed sentence to next Session. I was sent to Brixton Prison.

On the 9th or 10th July John Smith was brought there.

I was released on the 19th July. I have since seen the two German women, and they declare that they told the police that John Smith and I had different voices, that Smith was stouter and had a scar and a wart. The police said, "Never mind that; you have got the right man there."

HOME OFFICE MINUTE, DATED THE 23RD JULY, 1904.

CASE OF ADOLF BECK.

The history of this case is as follows:

In 1877 a series of frauds on prostitutes took place. In each case a man called on a prostitute, said he was a wealthy lord, wanted her to live with him or go yatching with him, said she required better clothes, gave her to purchase them a cheque for a large sum, signed illegibly, said he wished to give her a new ring, and borrowed a ring from her as a pattern, and having gone off with the ring, disappeared. A German named Weiss was convicted of these frauds in the name of John Smith. He was undoubtedly guilty, and served a term of five years.

In 1895 a series of exactly similar frauds occurred, about 50 women were defrauded. One of the women walking in Victoria Street saw a man whom she believed to be the swindler, and gave him in charge. This man was Adolf Beck. Of 22 women brought to see him, 10 positively identified him as the swindler; of the others some were uncertain, and one at least said that he was not the man. The police believed him to be the same person as John Smith of 1877, and he was tried on 10 charges of fraud. The theory of the prosecution was that he was the same person as John Smith whose *modus operandi* was precisely similar, and whose writing on the cheques and notes was identical, but this was not actually proved at the trial. The defence would have been that the frauds of 1895 must have been committed by the John Smith of 1877, but that Beck was not Smith, and they were ready to prove that Beck was in South America when Smith was convicted and imprisoned in England. The Common Serjeant (Sir Forrest Fulton) refused to allow the defence to give evidence for this purpose, and as the count charging Beck with Smith's previous convictions was dropped by the prosecution, the question whether Beck was Smith was not tried. Beck was convicted on the evidence (1) of 10 women who swore positively that he was the man who had swindled them, and (2) on the evidence of Gurrin, the expert, who said that the writing on the cheques and notes given by the swindler was that of Beck disguised. Beck was sentenced to seven years' penal servitude. While he was in prison he constantly asserted that he was not John Smith, and that he was innocent of the frauds of 1895. The question of his identity with John Smith was inquired into by the Home Office in 1898, and his description and marks were compared with those of John Smith now brought forward for the first time. They were found not to correspond, and in particular it was found that Smith was circumcised, while Beck was not. The Home Office decided that Beck was not John Smith, and Smith's name and conviction was erased from his penal record. Sir Forrest Fulton, who was consulted, advised that the question whether he was Smith or not was immaterial; the point, he said, had been excluded at the trial, and Beck had been convicted of the 1895 frauds by overwhelming evidence. His petition for release was therefore refused. In 1901 Beck was released on licence, when he had served his full time. In 1904 frauds on prostitutes recommenced, the *modus operandi* being exactly as before. The police told one of the women to stand in Tottenham Court Road, near the place where Beck was lodging, and, as he went in the morning to the City, she identified him as the person who swindled her and gave him in charge. All the five women who had been defrauded picked him out and identified him. He was tried at the Central Criminal Court in May, and on the evidence of the five women and of Gurrin, who again said the swindler's writing was of that of Beck disguised, he was convicted, but sentence was deferred until the July Sessions of the Central Criminal Court. While in prison awaiting sentence another case of fraud occurred, the swindler following the same device. He obtained two rings from two girls of the name of Turner, but their suspicions being aroused, he was followed and arrested while pawning the rings. This man's guilt, in this case, where he was arrested in the act, and in another case, where he stole an umbrella, which was found on him when arrested, is beyond doubt. He gave his name as William Thomas, but he has been identified, also beyond doubt, as the John Smith of 1877. It is now established very clearly that this man John Smith and not Adolph Beck is the swindler in all the 1904 frauds. (1) The *modus operandi* in all these frauds was the same as in the case in which he was taken in the act. (2) The handwriting in all the cases is undoubtedly that of John Smith. Mr. Gurrin has now unreservedly withdrawn his opinion that it is the writing of Beck. (3) Of the five women who identified Beck as the swindler two are abroad, but the other three admit their mistake and identify Smith as the swindler. Two of them picked him out without any hesitation from a large number of men. (4) One of the women in her evidence had stated that the man who swindled her had a gold watch with a number of Egyptian coins attached. This watch was not found on Beck, but it has been found on Smith. (5) The hotel notepaper used by the swindler has been found in Smith's possession.

As regards the 1896 frauds, there is also every reason to believe that Smith was the swindler, and that Beck is entirely innocent. (1) The women who identified him cannot now be traced, but it is reasonable to suppose that the similarity in appearance which led to his wrongful conviction in 1904 caused a similar mistake in 1896. (2) Gurrin withdraws his evidence. He says that the handwriting is not that of Beck. (3) One of the witnesses in 1896 said that the swindler had a prominent mark on the chin. This mark she was unable to find on Beck at the trial, but it can now be seen on Smith. (4) Mr. Macnaghten has seen one of the women who was defrauded in 1895. When confronted with Beck in 1896, she said he was not the man, and was not called as a witness, but now, on being shown some photographs, including Smith's, she at once, and without hesitation, picked him out as the man who had defrauded her. It appears to be established beyond all possibility of doubt that Beck was wrongfully identified as the swindler in 1896, and is innocent of the crimes for which he served a sentence of seven years' penal servitude.

C. E. T.
23–7–04.

[NOTE.–On the 29th July, 1904, Free Pardons were issued to Mr. Beck in respect of the 1896 and the 1904 convictions.]

–REPORT OF THE CASE OF WILLIAM THOMAS, ALIAS JOHN SMITH CONTAINED IN THE "TIMES" NEWSPAPER, OF 16TH SEPT., 1904.

CENTRAL CRIMINAL COURT, Sept. 15.

Before Mr. Justice Phillimore.

William Thomas, 65, journalist, who pleaded. "Guilty" yesterday to indictments charging him with stealing rings, the property of Nellie O'Neil, Violet Turner, and Beulah Turner, and an umbrella, the property of Nellie O'Neill, and to converting the rings to his own use and benefit, was brought up for judgment.

The prisoner also pleaded "Guilty" yesterday to a previous conviction in May, 1877 in the name of John Smith.

MR. JUSTICE PHILLIMORE, addressing the prisoner, said:–William Thomas, you have pleaded "Guilty" to three charges of larceny of a very mean and despicable character from three women, and to attempts of the same description which did not fail by reason of any repentance on your part. You have also pleaded "Guilty" to having been convicted of similar crime on or about May 10, 1877, on which count the Judge who presided at your trial awarded you a sentence of five years' penal servitude. It is suggested on behalf of the Crown that we have by no means got to the bottom of your offences when I state what I have stated.

It is suggested that it is at least probable that you were the author of 11 offences which were committed from December, 1894, to November, 1895, for which one Adolf Beck was tried, convicted, and sentenced, it is now thought unjustly; and certainly if you were the author of those offences it is certain that he was unjustly convicted. It is suggested, further, that you were the author of five offences in August, 1903, and February and March of this year for which Adolf Beck was again tried, before Mr. Justice Grantham, in June of this year, and was again convicted; but fortunately, owing to the care which my brother took before passing sentence, no sentence was passed. If you were the author of either or both these sets of crimes you are very bad indeed, and you have added to your offences by allowing an innocent man to suffer in your stead. I cannot help thinking that, at any rate as regards the later series of offences, they very closely correspond with the time when you were in London. I cannot help thinking that you are the real person who was guilty of those offences. There is no reason particularly that I see for supposing that you were the author of the earlier series of offences except that you were in London and that you in your first confession concealed the fact that you were in London at that time—and one would hope that there were not two people living at the same time who were guilty of this particular mean and, I am glad to say, novel form of fraud. I say there is no reason otherwise to say that you are the man; but with regard to both of the sets of offences for which Adolf Beck was tried I do not propose for one moment to consider that it is sufficiently proved before me that you were guilty of them to make me add one day to the sentence which I should otherwise have passed upon you. It would not be proper that I should, without full inquiry and full proof. I have only allowed counsel for the Crown to make the statement which he has made because it was in the nature of a justification of the character of Adolf Beck, not because it was to injure you, but because it was a convenient moment for making a clear statement with regard to a man whom the Crown believe to have been unjustly convicted. That being the case, I treat you merely as I should any one else who many, many years ago was convicted of this mean form of crime and who had a very severe sentence, which ought to have been a lesson to him, but who was found in his old age returning to his old wicked practices. The sentence upon you is the same as the previous one—that you be kept in penal servitude for five years.

A

DOCUMENTS GIVEN IN EVIDENCE IN THE CASE OF

R. v. JOHN SMITH.

1877.

1   *Letter written by John Smith to Ada Wooding.*
7 March 1877. see Appendix p. 227.

2   *"Cheque" given by John Smith to Ada Wooding.*
8th March 1877 see Appendix p. 227.

3   *Request to Messrs Howell & James given by John Smith to Ada Wooding.*
8th March 1877 see Appendix p. 227.

4   *Letter written by John Smith to Louisa Victoria Howard.*
18th April 1877 see Appendix p. 229.

5   *"Cheque" given by John Smith to Louisa Victoria Howard.*
18th April 1877. see Appedix p. 229.

1. Letter written by John Smith to Ada Wooding
7th March 1877

The Army and Navy Club
Pall-Mall
Wednesday afternoon

My dear Mrs Wooding,

Will you please expect me to-morrow
(Thursday) at two o'clock. —

yours

Captain JWS

2. "Cheque" given by John Smith to Ada Woodrug 8th March 1877

3. Request to Mess.ʳˢ Howell & James given by John Smith to Ada Wooding 8.ᵗʰ March 1877

Thursday 8th March 1877

Lord Willoughby desires Messrs Howell and James to provide the bearer of this letter with such dresses, Underlinen, &c, &c, as she may please to order, and put it to his account. —

4. Letter written by John Smith to Louisa Victoria Howard.
18.ᵗʰ April 1877

The Army and Navy Club
Pall-Mall
Wednesday Evening

My dear Mrs Beaumont,

Will you please expect me to
morrow (Thursday) at two o'
clock. —

yours

Major M

5. "Cheque" given by John Smith to Louisa Victoria Howard 19th April 1877 see p. 229.

London April 19th 1877

At Sight Months after date pay to Bearer order

Thirteen Pounds ten shillings

Value received.

To the Bank of London
19 Lombard Street

N. BARWISE & Co
Nº 3
MANUFACTURING
STATIONERS,
ST ANNS LANE
G.S.P.

B

DOCUMENTS GIVEN IN EVIDENCE IN THE CASE OF

R. v ADOLF BECK .

1896

1   *List of Clothes received by Daisy Grant, 5ᵗʰ July 1895.*
    see Appendix pp 239, 240, 263.

2   *"Cheque" received by Daisy Grant, 5ᵗʰ July 1895.*
    see Appendix pp 239, 240, 263.

3   *Letter received by Fanny Nutt, 3ʳᵈ December 1894.*
    see Appendix pp. 248, 255.

4   *"Cheque" received by Fanny Nutt, 3ʳᵈ December 1894,*
    see Appendix pp. 248, 255.

1, List of Clothes received by Daisy Grant, 5th July 1895.

A:℀   Redferns'

2 tailor made costumes
2 afternoon dresses
2 evening dresses
1 teagown
1 dressing gown   £15.v.v.
1 operacloak
1 cape
hats & bonnets
    corsets

Cobb. Barker street
    habit   £5.v.v.

boots & shoes   £5.v.v.

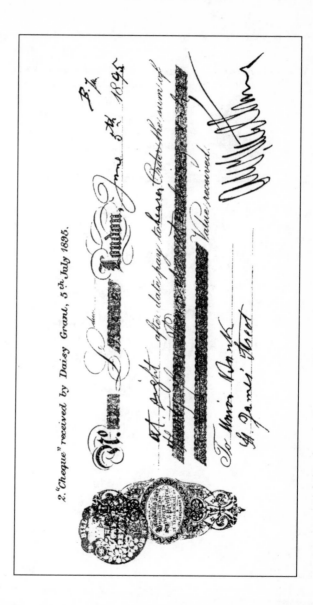

2. "Cheque" received by Daisy Grant, 5th July 1895.

3. Letter received by Fanny Nutt, 3rd December 1894.

GRAND HOTEL.

LONDON, _____ 189___
W.C.

THE GORDON HOTELS, LIMITED.

Monday Evening

My dear Mrs Nutt

Please expect me
(to-morrow) Tuesday between
one and two o'clock. —

Yours

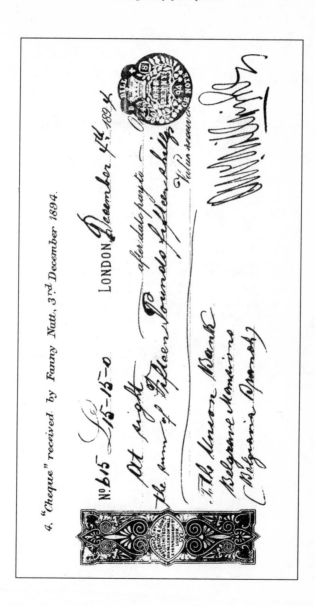

4. *"Cheque" received by Fanny Nutt, 3rd December 1894.*

C

DOCUMENTS GIVEN IN EVIDENCE IN THE CASE OF

R.v. ADOLF BECK.

1904.

1 *Letter received by Pauline Scott, 23rd March 1904.
see Appendix p. 302.*

2 *Cheque received by Pauline Scott, 23rd March 1904.
see Appendix p. 302.*

3 *Cheque received by Lily King, 29th March 1904.
see Appendix p. 303.*

4 *Letter received by Caroline Singer, March 1904.
see Appendix p. 304.*

1 *Letter received by Pauline Scott 23rd March 1904*

HⱵ⧸

HYDE PARK HOTEL,
ALBERT GATE,
LONDON, S.W.

Tuesday Evening

My dear Miss Scott,

I shall have pleasure calling to morrow (Wednesday) between one and two o'clock. —

Yours

[signature]

2. Cheque received by Pauline Scott 23rd March 1904.

March 23d '04

Pay bearer £ 120.0.0 pay One hundred
and twenty Pounds sterling in cash.

The Union Bank
Pall Mall.

3. *Cheque received by Lily King* 29th *March* 1904

No account

5ª/ No.   March 29th '04

Pay bearer £250.0.0. pay Two
hundred and fifty Pounds sterlg

the Union Bank
26 Knights Bridge   Lily King

4 *Letter received by Caroline Singer, March 1904*

HYDE PARK HOTEL,
ALBERT GATE,
LONDON, S.W.

Saturday

My dear Miss Singers,

will you please
expect me tomorrow (Sunday)
between 12 and 1 o'clock. —

yours,

D

DOCUMENTS GIVEN IN EVIDENCE IN THE CASE OF

R.v. WILLIAM THOMAS ALIAS JOHN SMITH 1904

1. *Letter received by Beulah Turner 7th July 1904.*
   see Appendix p. 312.

2. *List of clothes received by Violet Turner 7th July 1904.*
   see Appendix p. 311

1. *Letter received by Beulah Turner 7th July 1904*

HYDE PARK HOTEL,
ALBERT GATE,
LONDON, S.W.

Wednesday

Dear Madam,

Please expect
me to morrow (Thursday)
between 12 and 1 o'clock

Yours

[signature]

2. List of clothes received by Violet Turner 7th July 1904.

2 + lemonade dresses 20, 0,0
2 afternoon a 10,0,0
2 evening i 20, 0,0
1 tea gown 5, 0,0
1 .... i 2, 0,0
underwear 20, 0,0
Hats 5, 0,0
Boots a shoes 5, 0,0
extras 3 . 0,0
tailormade dress ....
....

E

DOCUMENTS IN THE HANDWRITING OF

Mr. ADOLF BECK

1. *Letter written by Mr Adolf Beck to Mr G. Chetwynd 4th April 1895. see Appendix p. 265.*

2. *Letter written by Mr Adolf Beck to Mr G. Chetwynd 21st March 1895. see Appendix p. 265.*

3. *Telegram written by Mr Adolf Beck after his arrest on the 15th April 1904. see Appendix p. 306.*

1. Letter written by Mr. Adolf Beck to Mr. G. Chetwynd: 4th April 1895

Buckingham St
Strand
4 . 4 . 95

G. Chetwynd Esq

Dear Sir

I am sorry it is
impossible for me to
call on you at 11-30
tomorrow – as I have
several prior appointments
from 10 to 3. p m –
but shall be pleased
to do so at my
earliest opportunity

Yours faithfully
A Beck

2. Letter written by Mr Adolf Beck to Mr G. Chetwynd. 21st March 1895

Buckingham Hotel, Strand
London 21st March 95

Mr G. J. B. Chetwynd
Sir
      In further reply to your letter
of 19th inst. I may say, it was
not my intention to hurt your
susceptibilityes —— In saying
that if that Party from whom you
had unsolicited communications
in regards to my property— was
anything like those I met thro
you before — it would be useless—
as none of them did anything
but waste valuable time —
this you know to be perfectly
true —— and in asking you
for an interview to discuss
with _you_ Matters — it was-

3. *Telegram written by M. Adolf Beck after his arrest, on the 15 April 1904*

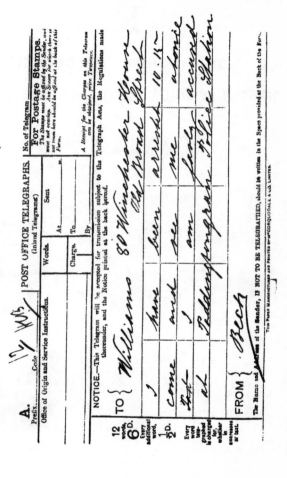

A. Prefix........Code........ 1/2 W/S

POST OFFICE TELEGRAPHS.
(Inland Telegram)

Office of Origin and Service Instructions.

	Words.	Sent
		At........ M.
Charge.	To........
		By........

No. of Telegram........

For Postage Stamps.
The Stamps must be affixed by the Sender, and must not overlap. Any Stamp for which there is not room here should be affixed at the back of this Form.

A Receipt for the Charge on this Telegram can be obtained, price Twopence.

NOTICE.—This Telegram will be accepted for transmission subject to the Telegraph Acts, the Regulations made thereunder, and the Notice printed at the back hereof.

12 words. 6D.
Every additional word, 1/2D.

TO { Williams 80 Winchester House Old Broad Street

I have been arrested 10.15

come and see me atonie
but I am falsely accused
at Bishopsgate Police Station

FROM { Beck

Every word tele-graphed for, whether in sentences or not.

The Name and Address of the Sender, IF NOT TO BE TELEGRAPHED, should be written in the Space provided at the Back of the Form.

THIS PAPER MANUFACTURED AND PRINTED BY M'CORQUODALE & CO. LIMITED.

233

F

PETITION TO THE HOME SECRETARY
WRITTEN BY JOHN SMITH 25TH JUNE 1879.

PETITION.

A 60 181

No. 413c

Register No. Q 523   Name _John Smith_

Confined in _Portsmouth_ Prison.

Date of Petition _25 June_ 1879

	Convicted		Sentence	Remarks
When		Where		
7 May 1874	Cent. Crim. Court	Larceny	5 years P.S.	Ml Marks forfeited

At Cross   Her Majesty

To the Right Honourable
Principal Secretary of State for the Home Department.

The Petition of _Jno Smith_ a Prisoner in the _Convict Prison_

HUMBLY SHEWETH—

The most respectfully undersigned was
tried at the Old Bailey in London for
Larceny at the first May Sessions 1879
and sentenced to five years P.S.—

He his sentence is a very severe
one, and he was not sent for trial
on the charge for Larceny, but for
obtaining money by false pretences, he
begs most humbly for a reconsideration of
his case, and that he may be deem Deserving
of a remission of part of his sentence.—

He begs leave to support this his hum
Petition by the following extenuating cir
stances:- firstly: its being his first offe
2dly, the smallness of his amount
3ly, that more than half of his alot.
sentence has already expired, and his
his good behaviour during the past ter
of his imprisonment.—

John Smith

Other titles in the series

John Profumo and Christine Keeler, 1963

"The story must start with Stephen Ward, aged fifty. The son of a clergymen, by profession he was an osteopath … his skill was very considerable and he included among his patients many well-known people …Yet at the same time he was utterly immoral."

The Backdrop

The beginning of the '60s saw the publication of 'Lady Chatterley's Lover' and the dawn of sexual and social liberation as traditional morals began to be questioned and in some instances swept away.

The Book

In spite of the spiralling spate of recent political falls from grace, The Profumo Affair remains the biggest scandal ever to hit British politics. The Minister of War was found to be having an affair with a call girl who had associations with a Russian Naval Officer at the height of the Cold War. There are questions of cover-up, lies told to Parliament, bribery and stories sold to the newspapers. Lord Denningís superbly written report into the scandal describes with astonishment and fascinated revulsion the extraordinary sexual behaviour of the ruling classes. Orgies, naked bathing, sado-masochistic gatherings of the great and good and ministers and judges cavorting in masks are all uncovered.

ISBN 0 11 702402 3

The Loss of the Titanic, 1912

"From 'Mesabe' to 'Titanic' and all east bound ships. Ice report in Latitude 42N to 41.25N; Longitude 49 to 50.30W. Saw much Heavy Pack Ice and a great number of Large Icebergs. Also Field Ice. Weather good. Clear."

The Backdrop

The watchwords were 'bigger, better, faster, more luxurious' as builders of ocean-going vessels strove to outdo each other as they raced to capitalise on a new golden age of travel.

The Book

The story of the sinking of the Titanic, as told by the official enquiry, reveals some remarkable facts which have been lost in popular re-tellings of the story. A ship of the same line, only a few miles away from the Titanic as she sank, should have been able to rescue passengers, so why did this not happen? Readers of this fascinating report will discover that many such questions remain unanswered and that the full story of a tragedy which has entered into popular mythology has by no means been told.

ISBN 0 11 702403 1

Tragedy at Bethnal Green, 1943

"Immediately the alert was sounded a large number of people left their houses in the utmost haste for shelter. A great many were running. Two cinemas at least in the near vicinity disgorged a large number of people and at least three omnibuses set down their passengers outside the shelter."

The Backdrop
The beleaguered East End of London had born much of the brunt of the Blitz but, in 1943, four years into WW2, it seemed that the worst of the bombing was over.

The Book
The new unfinished tube station at Bethnal Green was one of the largest air raid shelters in London. After a warning siren sounded on March 3, 1943, there was a rush to the shelter. By 8.20pm, a matter of minutes after the alarm had sounded, 174 people lay dead, crushed trying to get into the tube station's booking hall. At the official enquiry, questions were asked about the behaviour of certain officials and whether the accident could have been prevented.

ISBN 0 11 702404 X

The Judgement of Nuremberg, 1946

"Efficient and enduring intimidation can only be achieved either by Capital Punishment or by measures by which the relatives of the criminal and the population do not know the fate of the criminal. This aim is achieved when the criminal is transferred to Germany."

The Backdrop

WW2 is over, there is a climate of jubilation and optimism as the Allies look to rebuilding Europe for the future but the perpetrators of Nazi War Crimes have yet to be reckoned with, and the full extent of their atrocities is as yet widely unknown.

The Book

Today, we have lived with the full knowledge of the extent of Nazi atrocities for over half a century and yet they still retain their power to shock. Imagine what it was like as they were being revealed in the full extent of their horror for the first time. In this book the Judges at the Nuremberg Trials take it in turn to describe the indictments handed down to the defendants and their crimes. The entire history, purpose and method of the Nazi party since its foundation in 1918 is revealed and described in chilling detail.

ISBN 0 11 702406 6

The Boer War: Ladysmith and Mafeking, 1900

"4th February – From General Sir. Redfers Buller to Field-Marshall Lord Roberts … I have today received your letter of 26 January. White keeps a stiff upper lip, but some of those under him are desponding. He calculates he has now 7000 effectives. They are eating their horses and have very little else. He expects to be attacked in force this week … "

The Backdrop

The Boer War is often regarded as one of the first truly modern wars, as the British Army, using traditional tactics, came close to being defeated by a Boer force which deployed what was almost a guerrilla strategy in punishing terrain.

The Book

Within weeks of the outbreak of fighting in South Africa, two sections of the British Army were besieged at Ladysmith and Mafeking. Split into two parts, the book begins with despatches describing the losses at Spion Kop on the way to rescue the garrison at Ladysmith, followed the army report as the siege was lifted. In the second part is Lord Baden Powell's account of the siege of Mafeking and how the soldiers and civilians coped with the hardship and waited for relief to arrive.

ISBN 0 11 702408 2

The British Invasion Tibet: Colonel Younghusband, 1904

"On the 13th January I paid ceremonial visit to the Tibetans at Guru, six miles further down the valley in order that by informal discussion might assure myself of their real attitude. There were present at the interview three monks and one general from Lhasa ... these monks were low-bred persons, insolent, rude and intensely hostile; the generals, on the other hand, were polite and well-bred."

The Backdrop

At the turn of the century, the British Empire was at its height, with its army in the forefront of the mission to bring what it saw as the tremendous civilising benefits of the British way of life to what it regarded as nations still languishing in the dark ages.

The Book

In 1901, a British Missionary Force under the leadership of Colonel Francis Younghusband crossed over the border from British India and invaded Tibet. Younghusband insisted on the presence of the Dalai Lama at meetings to give tribute to the British and their empire. The Dalai Lama merely replied that he must withdraw. Unable to tolerate such an insolent attitude, Younghusband marched forward and inflicted considerable defeats on the Tibetans in several onesided battles.

ISBN 0 11 702409 0

War 1914: Punishing the Serbs

" ... I said that this would make it easier for others such as Russia to counsel moderation in Belgrade. In fact, the more Austria could keep her demand within reasonable limits, and the stronger the justification she could produce for making any demands, the more chance there would be for smoothing things over. I hated the idea of a war between any of the Great Powers, and that any of them should be dragged into a war by Serbia would be detestable."

The Backdrop
In Europe before WW1, diplomacy between the Embassies was practised with a considered restraint and politeness which provided an ironic contrast to the momentous events transforming Europe forever.

The Book
Dealing with the fortnight leading up to the outbreak of the First World War, and mirroring recent events in Serbia to an astonishing extent. Some argued for immediate and decisive military action to punish Serbia for the murder of the Archduke Franz Ferdinand. Others pleaded that a war should not be fought over Serbia. The powers involved are by turn angry, conciliatory and, finally, warlike. Events take their course and history is changed.

ISBN 0 11 702410 4

War 1939: Dealing with Adolf Hitler

The Backdrop
As he presided over the rebuilding of a Germany shattered and humiliated after WW1, opinion as to Hitler and his intentions was divided and the question of whether his ultimate aim was military aggression by no means certain.

The Book
Sir Arthur Henderson, the British ambassador in Berlin in 1939 describes here, in his report to Parliament, the failure of his mission and the outbreak of war. He tells of his attempts to deal with both Hitler and von Ribbentrop to maintain peace and gives an account of the changes in German foreign policy regarding Poland.

ISBN 0 11 702411 2

The Strange Story of Adolph Beck

"He said he was Lord Winton de Willoughby. He asked why I lived alone in a flat. I said I had an income and wished to do so … Two or three hours after he had gone I missed some tigers' claws and the teeth of an animal mounted in silver with my monogram."

The Backdrop

The foggy streets of Edwardian London were alive with cads, swindlers and ladies of dubious reputation and all manner of lowlife who fed on human frailty.

The Book

In 1895, Adolph Beck was arrested and convicted of the crimes of deception and larceny. Using the alias Lord Winton de Willoughby, he had entered into the apartments of several ladies, some of whom preferred, for obvious reasons, not to give their names. The ladies gave evidence, as did a handwriting expert, and Mr Beck was imprisoned. But an utterly bizarre sequence of events culminated in a judge who declared that, since he could himself determine perfectly whether the accused is of the criminal classes, juries should never be allowed to decide the outcome of a trial. The account given here is of one of the strangest true stories in the entire British legal history.

ISBN 0 11 702414 7

Rillington Place

The Backdrop

The serial killer, or mass-murderer, is often seen as a creation of modern society but quiet killers, drawing no attention to themselves in the teeming streets of the metropolis, have been responsible for some of the most notorious crimes of the 20th century.

The Book

In 1949, Timothy Evans was hung for the self-confessed murder of his wife and daughter at 10 Rillington Place, Notting Hill but their bodies could not be found. Two years later, a couple moved into the same ground floor flat, vacated by a man named Christie. They discovered bodies in cupboards, Christie's wife under the floorboards and Evans wife and daughter in the garden shed. Christie was convicted of mass murder and hung. At two subsequent enquiries, it was suggested that Evans may not have been a murderer. So, why did he confess?

ISBN 0 11 702417 1

Wilfrid Blunt's Egyptian Garden : Fox-hunting in Cairo

"Cairo. July 23, 1901 – On Sunday morning a fox-hunt was taking place near Cairo, in the desert, the hounds following a scent crossed the boundary-wall of Mr. Wilfrid Blunt's property, and two of the field, being British officers, who were acting as whips, went in to turn them back. Mr. Blunt's watchmen surrounded them, and, although they explained their intention, treated them with considerable violence."

The Backdrop

In the days of Empire, the British way of life was carried on with a blithe disregard for local peculiarities and this went hand in hand with a sometimes benevolent, sometimes despotic, belief in the innate inferiority of those under its thumb.

The Book

In 1900, the Imperial British Army occupied Egypt and, in order to provide sport for the officers who were kicking their heels, a pack of hounds was shipped out from England to hunt the Egyptian fox. Unfortunately, the desert provides poor cover and, one day, the pack, followed in hot pursuit by the officers, found itself in the garden of the rich and eccentric poet Wilfrid Scarwen Blunt. Attempting to protect the absent Mr. Blunt's property, his servants tried to prevent the hunt and were promptly arrested. Mr. Blunt objected to the officer's behaviour, both to the government and the press and the matter became quite a scandal.

ISBN 0 11 702416 3

R101: Airship Disaster

" ... *about seven and a half hours later, shortly after two o'clock in the morning of October 5th, she came to earth two hundred and sixteen miles away in undulating country south of the town of Beauvais in France, and immediately became a blazing wreck. Of the fifty-four people on board, all but eight perished instantly in the flames ...* "

The Backdrop

In the golden age of air travel, the R101 was the biggest and most splendid airship in the world. On the evening of the 4th October 1930 she left her mooring mast at Cardington on her ill-fated journey to India. As the ship ploughed on through increasingly threatening weather The Air Minister and his guests retired to their well appointed cabins. Seven hours later at 2.05 am her burning frame lay shattered on a hillside in France, 46 its 54 passengers killed instantly. The high hopes and ambitions of a brief but glorious era in aviation perished with them in the flames, changing forever the way we would fly.

The Book

As the shocked nation mourned, a Court of Inquiry was set up to investigate the disaster. Its report exposed the public pressure from the Air Minister, Lord Thomson, that whatever the technical causes of the crash had at the last minute unduly hurried designers, constructors and crew alike. The early end of the airship in modern commercial flight was the result.

ISBN 0 11 702407 4